HABIB

the man who built an empire

Hritu Pawar

Published by
Renu Kaul Verma
Vitasta Publishing Pvt Ltd
2/15, Ansari Road, Daryaganj
New Delhi - 110 002
info@vitastapublishing.com

ISBN-978-93-82711-80-3

Cover and layout by Vits Press
Printed by Vikas Computer and Printers

CONTENTS

To my parents:
Asha and Ghanshyam Singh Pawar

ACKNOWLEDGEMENTS

I would like to acknowledge my husband, Mukul Gupta, for his unconditional love and support. I sincerely thank all my friends and family for their unconditional love throughout this project.

And, No Thanks to Shashiraj Oswal, for being the best critic and a great friend, inspiring me to keep the fire alive inside, and helping me to grow into a better human being.

I also thank Google, Wikipedia, all open sources for material that went into making of this book and all the media houses quoted here.

AUTHOR'S NOTE

She was the most beautiful creature on Earth
her hair said so in that language only hair can speak.

Gabriel Bá, Daytripper

Writing a biopic on a living legend, a pioneer in his field, seems easy at first glance, but my journey was not a piece of cake. Why so? Let me tell you. When I got the opportunity to write Habib Ahmed's story, I was very enthusiastic and full of energy. I thought I could easily gauge the ups and downs of his life which could be brownie points for the book. When I started talking with this legend, I found that this story is not a simple one, it has many shades. I immediately knew that it was going to challenge my skills.

The reason being that every event and story in this life had a link with another. You cannot separate one thread from the others, it is all related.
We often hear stories which start from the scratch and end at the top of the ladder of success. Habib saab's story is no different but it is a very inspiring story because of the many dimensions it encompasses.
For me this book is not a typical book in that sense. It is a process to understand the journey. The journey of a man who could be anyone because this story inspires us to take a few more steps towards fulfilling our dreams. His footsteps lead a simple story towards a great story because it is not related to only one person, it is the story of community emancipation, it is the tale of a fashion revolution and the transformations that have taken place in hundreds of peoples' lives after a haircut at Habibs. They are stories by themselves. So many, many can thus relate his or her struggle to this story.
Commenting on the typically Indian way of thinking and what a struggle it was to establish himself as an icon of a changing India, Habib Ahmed says, 'One should be aware of his, her looks before they make up their mind about changing their hair style. Styles have changed in India. During the Sixties and the Seventies, long hair was considered a mark of beauty among Indian women. Gradually, with Western

influence, Indian women decided to take the plunge and get a haircut. Many now feel that it is important to have a good hairstyle along with facial treatments.'

Jawed Habib, Habib Ahmed's famous son adds to this by explaining that hair style is a circle. The style goes round and round. 'A period of straight hair like Zeenat Aman's followed by a period of curls like Madhuri Dixit... then the semicircle of changing style and back to straight or curly, the full circle that keeps running and we think fashion is changing.'

Habib senior notes, 'Often I ask a person's surname and profession to understand his background and approach to life, for everybody can't handle experimentation.' Habib Ahmed shares a story where a lady gave him a free hand and when he came up with a new cut, she became so volatile that she threatened to commit suicide. 'She said she would put my name in the suicide note. That night I could not sleep. However, after a couple of days, she called up and apologised for her behaviour. At times, people take time to settle with a new hair cut.'

These nuggets of personal information from Habib saab show how we Indians think and live and how we are influenced by anything which is called a symbol of stature or so-called pride. Sometimes, I feel how small we are when we see the importance of such small matters. But at the same time, I feel proud that we are moving ahead with the changing times and other interests have begun to engage us more than looks and getups, which we take as a regular occurrence now in our daily strides on the journey called living.

I found Habib Ahmed a family man, full of love and care. He has a big family, but that's not all. 'My father has always tried to give us the best of comforts and opportunities in life. I remember, when he was working for the Oberois, he would devote all his free time on Mondays and Tuesday to his family. The three of us (Pervez, Amjad and I) would be bundled on to his Rajdoot and be treated to a round of movies, or a trip to the zoo or India Gate', recalls Jawed Habib, the Bollywood icon.

In those days, a cooler in the house was a luxury. Amjad, the youngest son, remembers that he wanted a air cooler in the house. Soon, there was the air cooler to tide over Delhi's hot summer. That was the time life began to become better gradually for the family. Habib was, however, vigilant about what was 'need' and what was luxury. He is a man who knows the value of every penny.

Amjad recalls that Habib used to give tasks to his children and when he came back home from work in the late evenings, he checked their progress. He was very keen to monitor the learning and education part of all his children. When Amjad was about eight years old, the family lived in East of Kailash.

Habib explains it thus, 'when I look back. I feel a twinge of regret, for what I could not give my sons in their growing years was my time. Initially, I was too busy trying to keep a roof over our heads and later, driven by my quest to be the best. What I have given them is a running business, where they walk in as the boss. Perhaps it is one of the reasons why their value for money is so different from mine.'

After so many years of a very successful journey in a very creative profession, Habib recognises the growth of India. He simply says that now we are at a plateau from where we can go forward and forward. Habib is surprised by this development. An open economy helps us to explore our skills and thoughts. He compares it to the many gears in our car. We understand what the limitation of the first gear is; when we see a smooth road, we change the gear and we get slightly more speed and as the situation develops and according to the road under us, we follow the rules of the gears, he says. But gears have their own limitations, he points out. We have to run and whizz past but we cannot hit anybody. At this stage of life Habib Ahmed is not fading away, he is strong and growing with many able hands to help him. The hands of his famous and skilled sons and his many students who are taking his name and fame to greater heights and using the skills he has imparted to build many things new and exciting.

Habib Ahmed always uses *sher* (poetic lines) to express his feeling about the many situations he faces and he also uses *sher* sometimes to make me understand problems and the philosophy of life.

Tarakki use kahte hain jake puchh us pathhar se,
Pade the to pathar the, tarasha to khuda nikle.
Go and ask the stone what is success, it was just a mere stone, But when it was carved, we found a God in it.

The Cutting Edge

Gabriel Bá, Daytripper's language of hair was heard by a young man from India in the 1970s and he became a master of the art of dealing with it. Habib Ahmed is a hair stylist who has held his shears with honour for five decades. The man who gave the Habibs brand its name, Habib Ahmed is an affable and soft-spoken person, who single-handedly spearheaded fashion hairstyling in India and took 'styling' to a new horizon, refining, redefining and revolutionising the concept and standards of creativity and dexterity in hair care in India. He has been honoured with the prestigious 'Indian International Gold Award, 1995' and the 'Pride of Country Award, 1999' for his outstanding excellence, meritorious individual achievements and distinguished service to the nation. Also, he is a life member of the World Federation of Supreme Hairdressing since 1968 and has

A Young Habib with Alfred Morris of Morris School

been on the panel of judges at numerous international beauty pageants and hair shows.

In him, 'Modern Hairstyling' and 'Habib's Hair Styles' have found an able ally. He has taken this fragile, hair-thin industry across the country to a luxurious growth, basking in the warmth of glorious snippets carefully scissored away. Those getting a hair cut from this legend feel on cloud nine and boast truckloads.

In keeping with the tradition of service with a difference, for the last three decades, HABIBS have carved a niche for themselves in the field of professional and creative hairstyling in India and overseas. Having introduced the idea of 'styling', Habibs have integrated hairstyling, beauty and personality grooming in India. Today, this is a brand whose concept of hairstyling is a perfect amalgam of Indian and Western hairstyling based on the Geometrical System. Their potential skills, aesthetic sensitivity and solid expertise help them to understand the clients' requirement better and do wonders with hair. Habibs spells professionalism and client satisfaction from all over the world. Their breathtaking achievements prove their excellence on all kinds of hair so you can be modest when you say you're in tune with the times by getting your hair cut at Habibs.

Habib Ahmed, founder of the 'Habibs' group of saloon chains and academies, was born on 2 October 1940 in the small town of Jalalabad, near Muzaffarnagar in Uttar Pradesh. It was a settlement of Afghans from the middle ages. He has

Habib with Mr Morris

six sisters and three brothers. Habib's father Nazir Ahmed was barber to the Viceroys of British India in its last years, Lord Linlithgow and Lord Mountbatten. He had joined the services of the British government in India around 1936 at the then Viceroy House. After India became independent, Nazir continued working for the Presidents who occupied the palace that came to be called the Rashtrapati Bhavan. His first President was Rajendra Prasad.

Habib went to England to study hair designing. He did not know how to react to this decision that came out of the blue from his father, and to this he could not say 'No'. He went to the UK in the '70s and his first love, football, grew distant. He studied and trained in London for several years at what is popularly known as the Morris School and returned to India with a new definition for the barber's profession, transforming the conservative image of a *nai* under the tree privy to deep dark confessions and a parlour king.

Once upon a time, the Morris School where Habib Ahmed and his sons trained, was one of, if not the first school of British hairdressing, set up by Adele Morris and her husband Alfred Morris. It was a time when the word 'hairdressing' really encompassed all that took place. The emphasis was on the use of waves and curls. Rows of hood hair dryers lined the saloon and there are photographs of the 1950s with rows of women under them 'when the sweet smell of setting lotions wafted in the air'. They tended their client by shampooing, setting the hair in rollers and placing them under the dryer for 20 mins. The dry hair was then dressed into style. By the 1970s Morris had become a name in styling and training.

After training in the UK, from 1971 to 1981 Habib worked with the Oberoi Group of Hotels in New Delhi, after which the vague thought of opening his own saloon became strong. Habib had the chance of training with famous European brand names Alexander, Mario and Bruno and now, what they had done in entrepreneurship was what Habib wanted to emulate in India. His name, his own styling outfit, his exclusive saloon under his ownership. In 1983, the first Habibs Hair & Beauty Saloon was set up in the Lodi Hotel. Within the next two years, Habib also set up a teaching institute for styling, Habib Sons Academy, which too operated from the same Lodi Hotel premises. Now, the House of Habibs is a well-known name in the hairdressing industry, with brand saloons in New Delhi, Mumbai, Kolkata, Udaipur, Jaipur, Hyderabad, Mangalore, Cochin, Goa, Bangladesh, Nepal, London and New York.

Habib Ahmed took over a traditional craft from his father Nazir and has been instrumental in revolutionising hairstyling in India. Habib's three sons—Jawed, Parvez and Amjad—are brand ambassadors in their own right and continuing the family business and are frequently on the move across India and abroad providing training to other hairstylists.

Habib Ahmed says that he is able to value the importance of his family, which include four grandchildren, and after all the effort that he has put in, he is glad that he can 'finally discuss hair styling not merely with his sons, but with his daughters-in-lawas well, which is a dream come true.' He discloses, 'While the children don't want to break away, I have suggested that we branch out differently on point of professional techniques.' That is the way to go he feels in modern times since the times have changed.

Son Jawed describes his father's success and motivation level, which he observed the most among his brothers, enthusiastically, 'What I really admire about my father is the fact that he is a genuine human being. He also has a wonderful ability to mould himself perfectly to the various roles life demands of him. So, while he is the attentive consultant with his clients, he is the adoring grandfather with my children and affectionate father-in-law to my wife.'

Hair styling is not just about geometrical proportion but is also about an individual's personality. Habib adopted the science of understanding and styling hair and not merely cutting or using styling products. Thus, Habibs today is a symbol of a science-based styling and not a products-based one. In this biography, Habib Ahmed shares with us the subtleties and nuances of hair texture, cosmetology and hair cutting he has treasured in the time span of more than fifty years.

There are strange rules of love. One who is in love, the one who understands love or who has learnt the lesson of love—that guy never gets off. He is riding a tiger and he will continue to ride it until the tiger falls dead. And hair is a tiger that grows in profusion and is not likely to ever fall dead; so the hair business will always flourish. Habib senior has a gold mine in his hand, a mine that never gets exhausted. As a business proposition, there could not have been a better product. And when Habib started his independent business in 1982, the timing was propitious. The country was India. He was among his own people. He knew their pulse. The numbers were always there and there could be nothing better than beginning work among his own people. The 'styling' concept was new in India and its place under the sun was yet to come. Good times ahead was the only way to go.

Brand Habib

Today Habib Ahmed stands tall as an achiever, a teacher, an entrepreneur.

The turning point came on a normal day in 1980, when least expected and the professional and householder, Habib Ahmed was doing his regular stuff at the Oberoi's saloon where he was master hairdresser and stylist. The client who walked in and wanted a hair cut from Habib was one Mr Sulemaan of Lodhi Hotel. During the accompanying chit chat on the barber's chair, he made a proposition to Habib. A business in partnership, with an independent Habib saloon in Lodhi Hotel premises.

Habib had never thought in this way, and Habib Ahmed gave serious thought to the proposition. He discussed the idea with Rajan Nanda and Anil Nanda (friends). He told them that he had a keen desire to start his own saloon but

Habib posing with his awards

that he did not have finances. He told his friends that he had a financer at last; someone was offering a 'partnership'. After listening to Habib, Anil Nanda said that he should not take the decision in a hurry. That Habib should wait for some more time and then start his own independent business. 'If you have one chair, it should be your own.' Habib took this wise advice positively and started working to give shape to his dream.

He really worked hard to manage the finances. He managed to get Rs 84,000 on credit basis from his close relative, Zameen, on some profit percentage basis, with payback in a year's time. Simultaneously, he was also in touch with Sulemaan of Lodhi Hotel, negotiating for place in the premise.

Habib, however, had to keep his plans a secret as he was still an employee at Oberois. The struggle for a place went on for sometime as there was no shop place available at Lodi at that time. Finallly, Sulemaan offered Habib one of the hotel's 'discount' rooms. Habib converted that into a saloon. Only after getting a place in Lodhi hotel, Habib was relaxed. His contract with the Oberois was coming to end, and his boss was anxious that Habib sign another contract of three years with the Oberois. Finally the day came when Habib decided that he did not want to sign another contract; it was his last day at the Oberoi. He was confident that he could take all his high profile clients to his own saloon, but the situation was very stressful as he

Prents, Nazir Ahmed and his wife Bashiran

Habib Ahmed and his wife

Habib Ahmed and his wife, with parents and sons

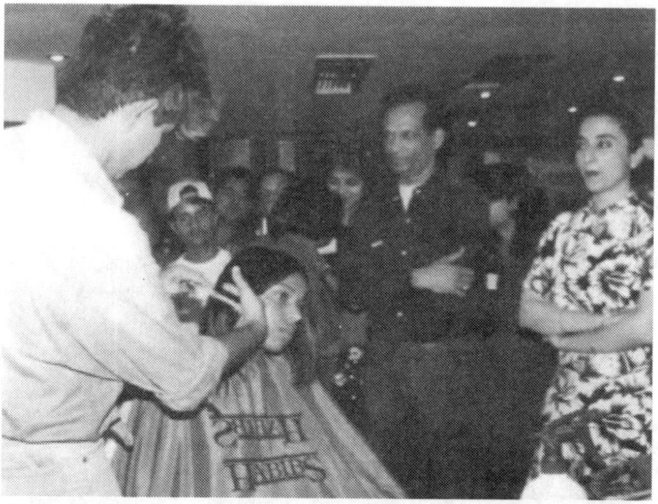

One of the Habib sons training in cuts and styles as the father keeps a watchful eye, sharing master tips

Jawed and Habib, father and son, graduates from Morris School. Seen here with a proud Morris

had to settle all his credit in a year's time. Time passed and his hard work paid and he was able settles the entire credit in six months time. Nevertheless, it was a tedious task to pull in the high-end clients like Gayatri Devi as Lodhi hotel then was a 3-star property. Habib, however, managed to get his elite clientele to his own saloon at Lodi.

Habib Ahmed's son Parvez has an anecdote to tell when anyone asks him how Brand Habib was built. 'As a child, I watched my father cut people's hair. He would always whisper, just for my ears, "*Aaye budhiya, jaye guriya*" (in comes a hag, out goes a babe). I was absolutely fascinated. I always wanted to be an artiste like Dad. Even today, when I accomplish a good cut, I remember Dad's whispered words.'

Sons. Sons, who were better educated and experts in their own right, form the bedrock of the empire that Habib Ahmed has built. Habibs.

Habib's youngest son Amjad says that, 'My father never gets off, because he knows what he is doing. He is in love with his work and art. He is still in love and passionate about cutting hair and he is still active as a stylist. That shows his commitment.'

The eldest of Habib Ahmed's sons, Jawed, himself a Bollywood success story, explains 'Brand Habib' in these words: If an Indian doctor can be famous and be recognised by developed countries, if a scientist can be honoured by big advanced nations, then why not an Indian hair dresser? I think my father feels a close relationship with hair, he

Sons. Sons, who were better educated and experts in their own right, form the bedrock of the empire that Habib Ahmed has built

talks to them, he tries to understand them. So, here we are. Habibs. Habib and Sons.

Recalling the early days, Jawed says, 'I saw my father on a cycle, going to the President's House, I saw my father on motorcycle, when he opened his first saloon in 1982 in Lodi Hotel. My father is a man with simple thoughts—that we have to move forward.'

Habib Ahmed has three sons with similar skills in hairdressing, but only one of them, Parvez, preferred to work with his father. Right from the start, the other two – Jawed and Amjad – branched out on their own, which led to a lot of talk about the brothers being rivals and not getting along. According to Amjad, there was never any family feud and it was all just a rumour. 'There was never any feud or animosity between me and Jawed. Who says so? The rumour that has been doing the rounds for so many years is that we are separate, but we never were. The fact is that my father has given us the freedom to do what we want and how we want to, so I have gone in my own direction and Jawed has gone in his. My father just thought that we have our own individual styles and should work our way up the ladder in our own capacities. Since we have such different styles and methods, there's always the chance of creative differences, and so our father thought we should work on our own.' But he does add that they were competing with each other earlier. 'We were competing with each other. We were one of the pioneers in the industry. Now, so many groups have come in. Because we were working separately, people have taken advantage of that. Now we work as one, as a united team', he says.

'Our father wanted us to work separately', Parvez, Habib's second son, confirms.

THE NAME

Amjad remember his father's smiling face when he started getting success. When the hard struggling days of the 1970s were replaced by the recognition of the '80s. Those were the days when hair styles or clothes designs from India didn't have much to share or much to say to the world. Fashionwise, only the West was acknowledged. Today things have changed completely. 'Today a film character cannot take final shape until and unless it is discussed with a hair stylist or designer. This is the change. Most of the film stars now follow that path of vision which my father was then trying to establish', he adds. By the '80s, Habib's fame had spread far and near and some big names started associating with 'only Habibs' as clients.

Habib always had in mind what his legacy was. That of a nai hajam, which in those days was thought to be a lowly vocation, caste and class. He always wished that he could have had a better education and a more congenial day-to-day living environment, although later in life he went to London for his study. But it was tough and he did not forget the poverty he suffered, having to work his way through college and training. Habib was a responsible father. The ghost of the bitter past was there, and he wanted to provide his own children with each and everything that he was far from getting during his own childhood, spent though it was in the premises of the Rashtrapati Bhavan.

Besides good education, career skills, expertise, experience and financial backing, Habib imparted to his sons professionalism, an unparalleled gift if you have to make a name and acquire fame. That is the mantra for a growing clientele which is the catchword for branding.

Amjad tells us, his mother Hashmi always says that among all of Habib's children, Amjad was the luckiest, 'because when I was born, the economic situation of the family started improving'.

Maqtabe Ishq ke dastoor nirala dekha,
Usko chhutti na mili jisne sabak yaad kiya.

Amjad is a dreamer and dreams big. It is he who brought to India the idea of hair colouring, highlighting, doing different, and being different, startlingly so at times for people with Asiatic features.

Amjad started working with his father in the Habibs while still a schoolboy. 'He (Habib senior) was not my father when he was in the saloon; he was Mr Habib. We brothers, his apprentices to begin with, were all instructed to call him Mr Habib and not Father. He was a thorough professional at work', says Amjad. In the initial days he treated me like any other fresher. I used to be a cleaning boy, a shampoo boy and helper... just like any other apprentice in the saloon. He was not ready to accept me as a son. Sometime I felt bad, but as I grew up I understood, that was how he was helping me to learn.'

'My father started from scratch and built an institution and he wanted us to go through the whole process. I understood that luck and skill play a part in success, but consistent progress requires more than luck or skill alone. The race does not always go to the swift or the fight to the strong, but, over the long run, to the one who is persistent.'

The family situation had the potential for Amjad and his brothers to be spoilt because, when they were at an adolescent age, their father was already an established name. 'But my father handled me and my brothers very well. He made us believe that he was always there to guide us. Some time he had no hesitation in reprimanding us, but he also kept a close eye on us and monitored our every need, which included the pocket money. He was strict with us but was not a dictator. On the professional front, many times he protected us by taking the blame when customers were irate and when any unpleasant situation occurred.'

When Amjad completed a few months at the saloon at basic jobs like cleaning and shampooing, his father told him to go to London to take a formal training. Jawed was already there. Clearly, Habib wanted a tradition to continue. And he knew what a formal training can deliver for a boy like Jawed or Amjad.

When Amjad came back to India after studying cosmetology, he joined Habibs and asked his father to guide him and teach him how to catch clients. 'In the early days, even when I started, getting clients was not easy', Amjad says.

'One day I was depressed with my performance—that I was not able to attract clients—and then my father decided to talk to me and told me, "Why don't you snatch my clients?"' Amjad remembers how shocked he was that Habib senior was telling him to snatch clients from his father. 'But now I know what his vision was. A vision that makes me strong and confident.'

'We brothers have made our own names in this field now, but reality is that we didn't face any hard life and failures. The tree and the seeds were already there. We just helped to grow as branches. Our father had already planned and here his vision comes on the scene. He was very well connected with the western world and for us, we just had to explore the sky. Today, even at this stage, if you ask me to compare my success with my father's, it is just two per cent of it, just a fraction of that success which my father has achieved', says Amjad, the proud son.

Parvez, a designer par excellence, believes in the total look. He aspires to international fame and though usual in workstyle and his idea, Parvez is the most rooted in the parent organisation. He manages the Habibs saloon and Hair Academy for the deprived and the physically challenged at their Sainik Farms campus. He is the son always with Habib Ahmed, standing by his father.

THE FAME

'The son of a barber who built a Rs 300-crore empire' was the banner headline of a news portal not too long ago. Everybody can see that the emphasis was on the son, who moved away from the father and built a Rs 300-crore business empire. The media still said that the father is a barber and not a hair stylist. (The son of a barber who built a Rs 300-crore empire: rediff.com: 08 July 2013.) The fact is that our generation, the generation the writer belongs to, first heard the name of Jawed Habib before that of the senior Habib. Today's generation easily connects with Jawed.

One sees the power of the mass media, which said, Renowned hair stylist Jawed Habib was inspired to start a saloon while working at a McDonald's outlet in London. The story said, 'He (Jawed) is a graduate in French literature, but now he hardly finds any time for prose or poetry—because he is busy travelling across different cities in India training people on how to cut hair, telling them about hair styling, looking good and feeling good. Jawed Habib is today a well-known figure in the beauty business, but when he started out in the industry, hair cutting or being a barber was anything but glamorous.'

Jawed is a familiar name in the fashion and glamour milieu. His association with the Lakme India Fashion Week for the last many years and with Femina Miss India and the Panasonic hair care products has helped him create a niche for himself in a fiercely competitive world. He spearheads

the Habibs saloon chain and is a tireless worker, jetsetting from one city to another, sharing hairstyling tips and snipping his way to fame. Known for his futuristic cuts and vibrant colours, Jawed is also a Sunsilk hair expert and a familiar face on television.

Yet, the truth is, it was his father, Habib Ahmed who made the world of difference for Jawed and his brothers.

When I asked Habib senior about his eldest son, he told us, 'When I started working as a hairstylist, our profession had no respectability whatsoever. We were treated as glorified nais even though my clients were Indira Gandhi, the Oberois, the Modis and Rajmata Gayatri Devi. I had to struggle a lot to create awareness about international hairstyling trends and to earn respectability as a stylist. Even though I was treading an uphill and lonely path, I never forced my opinions on my sons, giving them all the freedom to choose their own course in life. And so, when I realised that Jawed had very little interest in my profession, I didn't really pressure him to take it up.'

However, 'my other sons, especially Parvez, were very keen and whenever they had free time, they would drop in at my saloon and watch me work. Jawed, on the other hand, wouldn't even touch the scissors or give my clients a second look. He was always a strong-willed boy, even though I could feel that he wasn't very confident about his career. While he was studying French for his Master's degree, I could see that he wasn't really sure of what to do with his qualifications in the future.'

Jawed explains the difference, 'Since, my father and I are from two very different generations, we do have our little clashes. While my dad believes that hairstyling is an art, I think it's a science. He thinks, it's all about being creative, while I believe it's all about a mathematical approach. What's more, while he believes in treading cautiously, I believe in living for today. Who knows what's going to happen tomorrow?'

These ideological differences are but normal in any family that's into a common business. 'What matters is that my father and I are more like friends today. My father is an extremely down-to-earth person and we work as a very cohesive and successful team. And in this team, there is ample space for each one of us to work the way we want, while never losing sight of our common goal', says Jawed.

Habib senior explains, 'There essentially has to be a difference between the way my sons and I think. But there's a compromise, which is a healthy way out for ironing out differences, whether it is about lifestyles or attitudes to highlighting, perming and other techniques in the profession.'

Habib Ahmed himself was very ambitious, he wanted to make his own path and to uplift the profession of hair cutting was his inner desire. In 1984 his academy began with only four students. In 1988 when Jawed joined Habib senior, he came up with the idea of seminars and schools in tier II cities and metros. Their target audience was all the *guli* (bylanes) parlours, to make the small shop-small town barbers more skilled service providers. Habib Ahmed and his son Parvez started hosting seminars on the technicalities of hairstyling in Delhi. When Jawed came up with the idea of seminars in B towns to provide technical education for the beauty industry, ie. beauty parlours in smaller towns, the idea caught on. It was a successful idea at that time when seminars were only held by doctors and engineers. Recalling the time, a nostalgic Jawed says, '*ek nai bhi seminar kar sakata hai*. The journey leads us to the successful empire where we have MBA people and advisors working under the brand.'

This workshop idea was very successful and made the Habibs, father and the sons, harbour high hopes and made all of them aggressive in business. Each one of them borrowed many ideas from the West.

Habib had seen the franchise idea in USA and he wanted to bring this idea to India. There are three standard models of franchise—COCO (Company-owned), FOFO (Franchise owned, franchise operated) and FOCO (Franchise owned, company operated).

First Habib senior started with COCO outlets, opening a second saloon in Agra. It was difficult to manage and execute the idea as it was on profit-sharing basis. Then he opted for the FOCO franchise structure and opened several saloons all over India. Today Habibs has become one of the most known and reputed saloon brands in India.

Habib Ahmed gave the industry of fashion a beautiful career in Hair and Beauty Cosmetology at the Habibs Hair Academy. And he has succeeded to a large extent in reducing the stigma attached to the word nai and made hair dressing a respectable calling. Earlier, Habibs lent their name to the franchisee on a 35:65 profit-sharing basis, with the franchisee bearing all expenses and providing infrastructure, the Habibs providing skill, training and expertise. Now it is on the FOCO model.

In the meanwhile, he has also introduced in the last few years his own signature line of hair care products in the 'Habibs' range. His three sons Jawed, Amjad and Parvez have carved out their own niche areas and excel in them. The father gave them a rock solid education in the science of hair and technology, and let them each realise their dreams. All the sons take the name of the father HABIB for their respective enterprises. The generation next is waiting in the wings meanwhile to take on; right now they are studying and garnering the requisite skills in the world of hair a nd beauty.

'I never thought that I can take up my father's profession; I did my Masters in the French language and was looking for a career in Hotel Management. But when I went to London and visited the Morris School of Cosmetology and saw what the potential of this art was, I smelt the business and strength of this field. Then I decided that I should go with my father's profession. I was certain that this could be a

McDonald-like success story. People initially laughed at me, saying it would be impossible to do. But my father, I and my brothers worked hard to achieve this goal. My father and we brothers are focused on the growth of the profession as a business. One can say that we are like a horse wearing blinkers, with just one direction. Grow', says Jawed.

Today Jawed has changed the definition of styling. 'I am fond of ideas, who can think that a nai can come up with an idea of IPO for hair saloons. But please take note, anyone can have an idea, but very few are there to pursue that. Just think that the population of this country is 1.25 billion, if we have all the people visiting our saloon just once, we can do a big business and for this we would need at least ten thousand saloons in the country. Can anyone imagine how big this dream is?', he told the media a few years ago. Moving beyond IPOs, Jawed Habib Hair & Beauty Ltd (JHHBL) now raises private funding from its existing investors. In the 1990s, Greenfield/Sparrow Hill Advisory were offering funding to Habib's business, Habib Ahmed was that big by then. 'Without guidance of my father, I cannot even think about this venture. A leader is considered great when he makes new ways for others, not only for himself', Jawed adds.

'Sky is the limit and my father is here to guide us', an ebullient Jawed says.

'Let's see… we are going to achieve even more surprising things. Everyone talks about developed foreign countries and their systems. Everyone talked about London and their professionalism, I have also been there. But I only learnt ABC of the art, how one is going to use these letters is up to us. My father did exactly this. He made his education from abroad create something more acceptable to our country, India. He understood that mere copy of foreign techniques and style will not bring acceptability or success.'

The turning point came when Jawed made a trip to France and England. 'One fine day he called up to say that he had enrolled at Morris International, the same institute where I had studied cosmetology years ago. He stood first in the institute and his career took a flying start from this point. Today, thanks to the media attention and his association with the glamour world, he has gained a lot in confidence', says the fond father. .

'Jawed is more of a showman, full of energy and ideas, but as is the problem with the younger generation, he wants instant results and lacks patience. I like to move cautiously with my options known well before going into any business venture. But I have never forced my ideas on my son. Even when Jawed married outside our community, I accepted his decision happily. Fact is, we work as a single unit, even though we may have very different ideas.'

Jawed confides, 'I never realised when exactly my father's genes started asserting themselves... I became besotted with the glamour associated with the profession when I went to France and England.'

'It also helped that our father did not harbour any expectations. Maybe, that's why even though I am the eldest, I was the last one to join his profession. But today, I am a lot more serious about my work.'

Of his father, Jawed says, 'My father taught me commitment for hard work; he always says that if you are ready to do hard work, nobody can stop you. India has changed now; the population of this country has become its strength. Now our lifestyle is changed, our thinking is changed. Everyone seems to have branded belongings, even branded hair cut.' Jawed uses professional combs, neck brushes, towels imported from Korea, the latest in the industry technology.

The outlook in the West was very different from how Indians perceived the fashion space in the 1990s and that was an opportunity Jawed spotted. 'When I started doing my workshops in 1986, people would come and ask me to teach them a Sadhana cut or a Dimple cut, educating them about things beyond this was very exciting', says Jawed.

How does the senior Habib take his son's unprecedented success? The father's eyes sparkle when he talks about Jawed. 'It is his destination, it is his hard work and more than anything else, it is Jawed's imagination and entrepreneurship. His success gives me great happiness and makes me very proud.'

THE CAMPAIGN

'We put *'purani' sharab* into new bottle, we created an environment for the business, we streamlined the Human Resource (HR) policy, we used Information Tecnology (IT) for networking and reaching out, for client interface and blossoming as a business', says Jawed Habib, a byword in Mumbai's film world, describing the success of Brand Habib.

In the early days of his entrepreneurship, Habib Ahmed realised that if anyone wanted to expand business, one needed to have not only expertise but had to have awareness about what is happening around the world and about the latest fashion trends. One remains relevant forever if he or she keeps updating himself or herself. Updating in terms of horizons of this thinking, in terms of techniques and in terms of the rules of engagement with the customer. Habib had this instinct to see the world in the future. He knew that he needed people who had the ability to expand the art of hair styling. Habib is a pioneer and he thought, who better than his sons to take his efforts forward. His three sons became his master tools and established Brand Habib and took it to another level of experience beyond just the esoteric.

Dealing with many customers is a different thing but what about other people? Habib saab shares a story with us. 'People get a photo clicked with me and that's enough to gain credibility in their city. Once, during a journey, I stopped at a small place in Punjab and saw my photo in a barber shop. I asked the guy who is that man? He said, you don't know him. He is the country's biggest name in hair styling.'

Amjad is right. The market trend for the hair cutting industry is one of consolidation, both for high-end stand-alone parlours, chain saloons as well as for the family held companies. The 'Indian Cosmetic Market Outlook 2018', portrays the current and future scenario of cosmetic industry in India. Cosmetics market, once female dominated, has started earning high revenues from male counterparts as well by catering to male-specific needs, especially in creams and lotions. The revenue generated through male cosmetic market has increased the total revenue of the young Indian cosmetic industry. This spells well for Habibs Cosmetics. The share of hair care market is maximum in the cosmetic industry, with hair oil being the dominant segment. In future, although hair oil is expected to remain the leading market product but hair colour will attain the fastest growth rate in the segment. Herbal cosmetic products are increasing foothold in the Indian cosmetics industry with the growing demand for natural products and awareness about their benefits among the population. It is expected that this high demand will be lead by Southern India, as the region is more inclined towards home-made natural cosmetic products, the report says. So, after all, Jawed was not wrong when he opened his first venture in Kochi, Kerala.

By 2017, the market of beauty and wellness is expected to reach Rs70,324 crore with CAGR of 14 per cent. Forecasts say by 2020 the value of this industry will go up to Rs 99,000 crore. People today have disposable incomes and can invest in looking good, men too are beauty and style-conscious and the lifestyle is rapidly changing. Habibs today has many competitors and the Habibs know that the solid ground Habib senior has provided can only survive as a consolidated vision of his three sons.

A January 2012 report by PricewaterhouseCoopers, or PwC, and the Federation of Indian Chambers of Commerce and Industry suggested that the industry could double in size in three years. While small-town India has huge potential for saloon chains, but going beyond them might mean lowering prices.

Besides Indian chains, global ones, such as Toni & Guy and Saks, are making their presence felt. While demand is no problem, what could stand in the way of Habibs saloon chain expansion is the lack of skilled stylists. To get around it, Habibs have their own academies, whose graduates start with salaries of Rs 10,000 to Rs 20,000 a month, plus commissions and tips.

During his period of struggle in the 1970s, Habib had heard of another famous name, Alexandre of Paris. Habib says, 'I thought I should work with him, but how? By chance, at that time, Maharani Gayatri Devi came to me and mentioned that she was going to Paris. I asked her, who does your hair in Paris? And she answered that Alexandre did. So I told her that I wanted to work with Alexandre and she said she'd see what she could do. In one month, she sent me a telegram saying that I should come as soon as possible. It was expensive, but I went.'

There is a famous saying that if you are with good people, automatically and unconsciously, you will get good habits and skills. Habib didn't know this but every now and then time led him to meet masters in his field. Thus, he went to Vidal Sassoon's in London and Mario and Bruno in Paris. He felt that hair styling was in their blood. 'Meeting with these icons made me serious about my profession', Habib says. Meeting with industry stalwarts also helped Habib understand the mantra of styling, how one should think and conceptualise styling. Fortune was on his way and his dream was being fulfilled due to many conducive circumstances.

How did his customers react, even in the '90s? 'It was annoying. You come to me for a style that will beautify you and you instruct me to leave the hair untouched. It is like an artist being told how to draw a line. They did not allow me the privilege of creating a new look. Look at the Indian heroines two decades ago—they had such long hair but they would never get them cut.'

'I went into the mind of the people through education', is Habib Ahmed's punchline, when asked how he managed the change in style and perception?

One learns throughout one's lifetime. Earlier, one heard of concepts like adult education and continuing education. Today life-long learning is considered to be for the entire cycle of the human being, right from being a child to the old age. Learning takes place not just at educational institutions but happens in our life process—in our relations, our surroundings and our social set up, at work, in our profession as well as during our free time. And the greatest lessons often come from informal interactions.

During his engagement in Oberoi Hotel, Habib was on a major learning spree. He applied for many courses to refine his skills and expertise further. But even if he wished, Habib couldn't afford to go out of the country with a meagre monthly salary of Rs 750 and do hair dressing workshops or new advanced courses. He had to sign a contract and borrow money to pursue his dream courses. Oberois' Mehra agreed to give him Rs 10,000 but with the condition that he had to sign a service bond of three years with her. Once, when Gayatri Devi wanted her hair cut, Habib was not available. She learnt that he was chasing greater learning and sent him a telegram, asking him how many courses he would like to do, even when he was so skilled.

Habib went on to do 17 advanced courses in various countries. Seventeen is a fairly large number and one wonders what made Habib do so many extra courses when any other person would have stopped with two or three. 'Studies are must', says Habib. 'A person should be fully qualified. Moreover, one learns new ideas, creations, and techniques.'

Alexandre was a very creative person. He didn't speak much English, but somehow Habib always managed to converse with him. His clientele included film stars like Elizabeth Taylor. 'When Alexandre asked me, you know so much, you have degrees, you have travelled so much, then why are you working for someone else? It got me thinking seriously. I came back to India and I decided to open my own saloon. But there were not enough trained and qualified people to provide the required services. I thought that in India we have such intelligent, educated and bright people, so why can't we be as good as the rest of the world? Why can't I raise the standards by starting a school?'

He also remembered, when he was in England on a business tour, he had met one of his teachers and asked him how Habib could send more and more Indian students to the Morris school for training? His teacher had looked very surprised and had said, 'what is need to come over here in England? Take the syllabus and start over there in India.' Habib had found the key. 'Yes', he said. 'This is a great idea.' Everybody wants to go abroad to work and settle but only through education and skills can one make way to success. 'In India most of the people don't think in this way, they work but they don't try to learn skills. This is our main shortcoming. Learn as much as you can', Habib Ahmed says. There is a process for success in every field. 'No matter who your opponent is, one day people will start to accept you.' In any success story, yes there are some stories of pain, but with time, they all turn into stories of respect and loyalty, Habib senior adds. During his thirteen-year stint at the Oberoi, Habib also got to travel to various countries where he met many foreign hairstylists. He suddenly discovered that among so many stylists, his talent was unique as well. At a meeting in New York, Alexandre (of Paris) told him, 'Are you stupid? Despite knowing so much you work for someone else.' This blunt reprimand from his teacher shook Habib completely and the thought of opening his own saloon became strong.

During his long passionate professional career Habib has fielded many questions regarding Indian and Western hair style. But his view is very clear. In an interview with a newspaper during mid 90's, he has repeated, 'Indians are conservative, their hair styles are very strict and formal. The Indian female prefers long hair because it depicts a well-bred background. Most Indian women are reluctant to get their hair cut short. Besides, the dresses they wear go well with long hair. European women are daring and independent. They can afford to get their hair styled and dyed according to their own liking. A good style first of all requires a good hair cut. Hair should be cut in such a way that whether the hair is dry or wet, set or not set, the fall of the hair should be same. A little blow drying helps to give the style the final touch.'

The old socialist mantra of 'rice in every bowl' has now been replaced with 'a cell phone in every hand'. The rising tide of affluence has given today's youth the advantages of technology and a range of opportunities that no generation before them had. Nor have they ever represented such a predominant section of Indian society.

Habib wants to bring home the latest techniques from the West and it is through video and cassettes that he hope to arouse awareness. With additional videotapes gradually becoming a way of life with several professionals, Habib's scintillating treatise on hairstyle will no doubt add to the growing number of careers with the master touch and complete professionalism. Video cassettes for hair styling, no one can beat this. Today it sounds like 'if you have any issues, go to YouTube and search/watch the relevant video. I'm sure you will find the correct video there'. It is innovation and it is a fine example of enterpreneurship.

In January-March 1999 Habibs introduced something that we can call a way forward and at that time media called this 'A cut above the Rest'. How many times does one want some particular hairstyle but the very idea of experimenting with one's own hair puts one off. Many hairstyles look good on you but you don't know which is the best, the result is frustration and uneasiness, especially in today's world where everyone is very conscious about the look and overall appearance. In search for that 'wanted' look you may go through several cuts; as someone has said, 'a hairstyle is the fastest way of looking a martie or a fool'. A haircut affects the entire personality. Of course, Habibs proclaimed they would help you look 'graceful'. And how, if you wondered, they could make you look at yourself in different style!

The Habibs, for the first time, brought to Delhi computerised hairstyling, where in seconds your image can change more than ten hairstyles right from the usual to the unusual. It is just a onetime process and after that you are sure for the rest of your life. Habib Ahmed says, 'before giving someone a style, I take three things into account: the cheek bone, the texture of the hair and the overall personality of the person'. Habib's techniques are now on the net. Many want to make this profession as skill-based as medicine or engineering, says Habib adding that hair cutting is a special job where science and art come together. Today Habib himself is a celebrity and his clients include royalties, film stars, industrialists and foreigners but for him, 'Every client who pays me is a VIP. I put my best out for everyone'.

THE BUSSINESS

Today, Habibs Hair & Beauty is a one-stop-shop for the ordinary as well as the extraordinary, for the housewife and the VIP, for the chic student and the grandfather, who was perhaps the first in the family to have come to Habibs in the 1980s. Habibs has integrated hairstyling, beauty and personality grooming. In India, Habibs is also the place which can keep the fashionistas posted on the latest international trends.

The Habibs parlour at South Extension is the only parlour directly owned by Habib Ahmed. A very popular fashion destination in Delhi, the parlour has an annual turnover of about Rs 1.5 crore. Habib senior and Parvez are often to be spotted here, catching up with old acquaintances, entertaining the media as well imparting an experience of a lifetime to a first timer. All the other 42 saloons and parlours in the country are operated as franchisees.

Having witnessed frequent changes in techniques and trends in the beauty industry, the company invests in training and supporting its franchisees. In order to maintain consistency in service delivery and quality, it regularly updates all its franchisees on the technology know-how and saloon management skills. Habibs has opened 50 new franchise-based saloons in West Bengal. Most of these saloons are in tier II and III cities like Durgapur, Asansol, Kharagpur, Siliguri, Anandpur, Havana and Narendrapur.

In the last few years, Habibs has also introduced their own signature line of hair care products in the Habibs range. Skin toners and refreshers, moisturisers, cleansing milk, sun-screen lotion, spa massage cream, oily hair shampoo, anti-frizz hair serum, conditioners, henna—Habibs Cosmetics Pvt Ltd provide them all. The company, with a factory now in Dehradun, started in Gurgaon in 1997.

Today, it has an annual turnover of Rs 10 crore.

Habib tells the story of Hakim Lukman, to explain his skin and hair products and their speciality. He emphasises how he is trying to bring to the common man a quality of cosmetic and herbal product for hair and skin that is 'natural' and without the harms of synthetics.

Once upon a time there was a famous traditional doctor called 'Hakim' Lukman. Hakim Lukman was known for his mastery in herbal medicine and identifying of every herb which could be used as a medicine. He was admired as a great doctor who could extract all information from a patient even without touching him and merely by seeing his eyes. Folklore has it that the Hakim was so good that that herbs spoke to him and told him of their healing qualities. Amazingly, in gardens and jungles, every plant he said, had a particular quality, some medicinal, some with other properties. This story, Habib says, shows that Hakim Lukman was a master at identifying the quality of every plant source. Habibs cosmetics have every product ingredient traditionally identified, Habib says.

Habibs Academies impart training to a thousand young hair dressers coming from different parts of the country every year. They give Hair and Beauty Cosmetology training in various cities which offer comprehensive course in Cosmetology and crash courses in Hair Styling. Besides the thriving institute in Delhi, two new academies have been set up in Kolkata and Hyderabad in 2016. To have premier facilities is somewhat of a challenge. But the Habibs are doing it. Teaching tier II India to be equally stylish as Mumbai and Delhi.

Habib often tells his students, 'understand that your hair is not an adornment in itself, but a frame for your face. It should be cut so that the cut complements the facial bone structure'. There is hush in the wake of this statement while the wide-eyed students silently absorb the implications of the little pearl of wisdom dropping so casually from the master. Yes. He places the art and craft in its perspective with these few priceless words. No one knows it better than Habib and no one can say it better.

'I do not believe in being selfish and teaching five per cent of what I know on the subject. Nobody knows everything. No one is master'—asserts the master artiste. It takes some time for a person to achieve a fair degree of mastery. 'Besides, you cannot become an artiste unless you are deeply involved in it', Habib senior says.

As a pioneer in India's beauty and hair business, Habibs aims to develop a platform for sustainable startup business, contributing to skill and employment generation, service to community and putting India on the global fashion map in this particular sector of the industry.

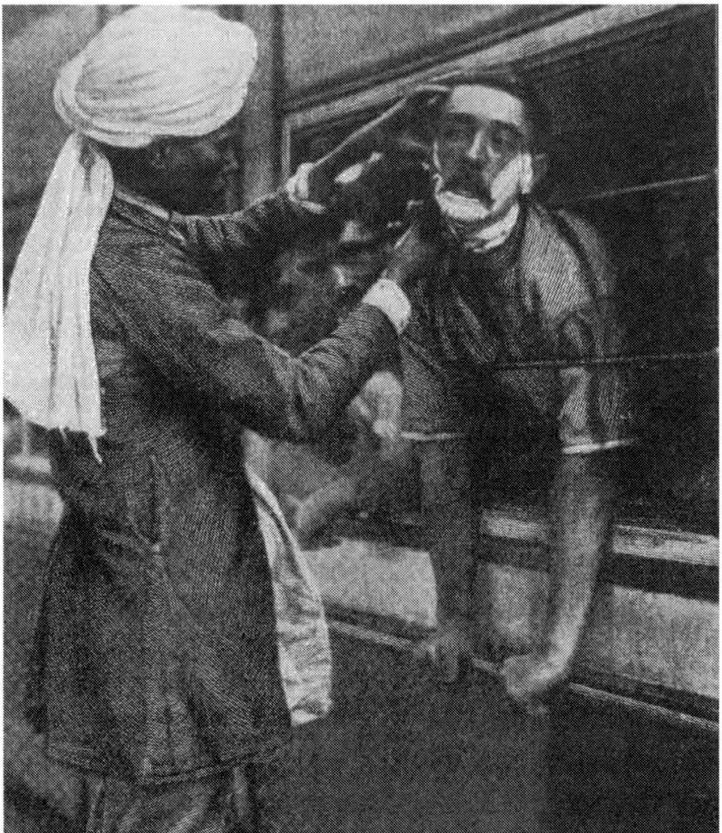

Yes! I am a Nai Hajam

Not many people can proudly say, Yes! I am a Nai Hajam. It takes immense courage to claim ownership of a community trodden under caste indignities for thousands of years. Yes, in India, the community of nai, hajjam, the barber, has a long long history of being looked down upon. And Habib Ahmed is a man not afraid of being labelled, he is a man who has brought not only dignity to the occupation but stature and respect to an oppressed community in a manner that no one can challenge. He has made himself a label, a brand, an identity that is world-renowned today for all the right reasons.

Yes, the inheritance is that of a nai, or a 'glorified nai', as he says, laughing. But what he has made of it is the big story. We need to look at the history of the community to gauge the magnitude of Habib senior's contribution to society.

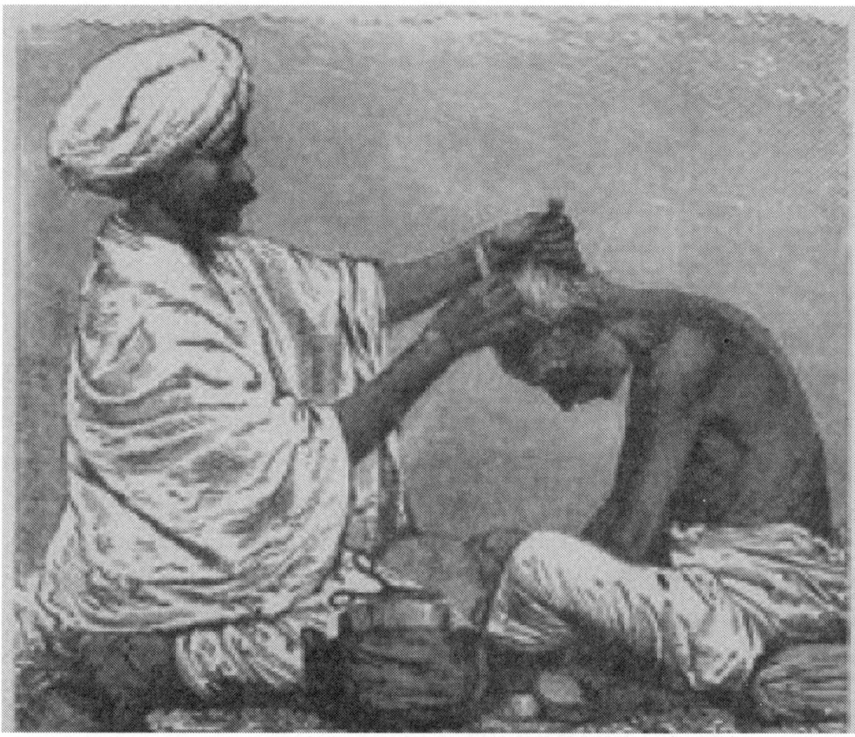

This is how barbers in India worked in the 19th century

This is an illustrations from the book India (1876), Part 2 of 2, which shows a typical street barber in the early 19th century. The lot of the barber was no different elsewhere in the world, as the Russian writer Anton Chekov describes in his famous story written between 1882-85.

Morning: It is not yet seven o'clock, but Makar Kuzmitch Blyostken's shop is already open. The barber himself, an unwashed, greasy, but foppishly dressed youth of three and twenty, is busy clearing up; there is really nothing to be cleared away, but he is perspiring with his exertions. In one place he polishes with a rag, in another he scrapes with his finger or catches a bug and brushes it off the wall. The barber's shop is small, narrow, and unclean. The log walls are hung with paper suggestive of a cabman's faded shirt. Between the two dingy, perspiring windows there is a thin, creaking, rickety door, above it, green from the damp, a bell which trembles and gives a sickly ring of itself without provocation. Glance into the looking-glass which hangs on one of the walls, and it distorts your countenance in all directions in the most merciless way! The shaving and haircutting is done before this looking-glass. On the little table, as greasy and unwashed as Makar Kuzmitch himself, there is everything: combs, scissors, razors, a ha'porth of wax for the moustache, a ha'porth of powder, a ha'porth of much watered eau de Cologne, and indeed the whole barber's shop is not worth more than fifteen kopecks.

There is a squeaking sound from the invalid bell and an elderly man in a tanned sheepskin and high felt overboots walks into the shop. His head and neck are wrapped in a woman's shawl.

This is Erast Ivanitch Yagodov, Makar Kuzmitch's godfather.

'How are you?'

'In a poor way, my boy. I've had a fever.'

'You don't say so! Fever!'

'Yes, I have been in bed a month; I thought I should die. I had extreme unction. Now my hair's coming out. The doctor says I must be shaved. He says the hair will grow again strong. And so, I thought, I'll go to Makar. Better to a relation than to anyone else. He will do it better and he won't take anything for it. It's rather far, that's true, but what of it? It's a walk.'

'I'll do it with pleasure. Please sit down.'

With a scrape of his foot Makar Kuzmitch indicates a chair.

Habib saab recalls reading a story by the famous writer Krishan Chander (1914-1977), where the protagonists are barbers. The father used to be called by the landlord to shave him. Others too called him, he waited to be 'called', his livelihood depended on being 'called'. The son, a young man, tells him one day, 'people will come to us'. Defying convention, he tells the father, 'we will set up a shop where people will walk in of their own volition and ask us to cut their hair and shave them.' It was a revolutionary thought even in the 1930s-1940s.

In a Lecture delivered on Urdu Literature by Javed Akhtar at Jamia Milia (translation by Humayun Zafar Zaidi), the poet-writer recapped Nazeer Akbarabadi's lines:

> *Marey hain hat hat pe sab yahan ke dastkar/Aur jitne peshadar hain rotey hain zar zar/Kootey hai tan lohar to peetey hai sar sunar/Khuch ek do key kam ka rona nahi hai yar/Chattees pesheywalon ka hai karobar band*
> (All the craftsmen are sitting idle/and all artisans are in tears/both the ironsmith and the goldsmith weep inconsolably/its not a problem affecting one or two/the business of thirty six professionals is at a standstill).

Javedji recalled that in a session of the Progressive Writers Association, Krishan Chander said:

> Its seems that our stories and poems barring few have not come down from the high pedestal. Poetry in particular has not yet outgrown feudal underpinnings... I do not find in poetry or other literary genres, the home and hearth of the poor nor the songs of the peasant, nor the workers endless travails. Our poetry does not refer to the working woman's broken comb with wisps of hair entangled in it; nor does it refer to Dabbo Manohar's pet that accompanies him every morning when he sets out to plough the fields; it does not reverberate with the sprightly and hold bold love songs which the rural women hum for their menfolk while carrying food for them across the uneven pathways. It does not allude to their clothes that smell of dung. Our literature has no reference to bathwa – it does not need to dwell upon the whiff of perfume

> emitted by the musk-deer nor the locks and tresses of Tataari beauties, and that is its major lacuna. I do not find the humble abodes of my country, its flora and fauna nor a familiar image that would enchant one even after a 100 years! Till such time that we do not come down to earth, and study the life lived by peasants and workers in their homes and paint its true picture with utmost sincerity and effort, till then our literature will not attain literary heights that will compel a reader in the world to conclude that Indians are the same as them. Though the task is difficult we have to accomplish it.

Javedji said, 'Krishan Chander alone could have said such things. I am convinced that there are innumerable people in India who have deeply felt the anguish of class struggle, social exploitation and inequality not as a consequence of a political leader's statement or an economist's discourse or a sociologist's thesis, but as an outcome of those progressive short stories that have shaped the readers' social consciousness.'

THE HISTORY

So, what have India's poets and writers been talking about? About occupations that are considered 'lowly'. Not only the sunhar and the lohar, it's the 'chattees peshewalon'—the tailor, the tinker, the shoemaker and, of course, the barber who have thousands of years of discrimination behind them. In an emerging India of the 1970s, Habib

Ahmed dared to defy these social girdles, break out of caste and class confines to establish the nai as the ideal hairstylist. Of course, he has competition, not only from multinationals like the reportedly 4,000 L'Oreal saloons but even the gods. The Tirupati Tirumala temple employs 600 barbers to shave hair of 20,000 devotees who visit the temple every day and 'offer' hair to the deity. Thousands of pilgrims sit cross-legged on the floor with their heads bent forward as the barbers work their razors at lighting speed. Folklore has it, Venkateswara or Krishna, of the Hindu Trinity, took a loan to get married. It was so huge, he is still paying it off and his devotees are helping him by giving their hair! Remember, Jawed Habib reminds us, India is a country of a billion people, the demographic advantage, and Habib Ahmed had the foresight to look beyond beliefs.

What Habib senior had to rise above is thousands of years of tradition. Chandan Gowda, writing in the newspaper, *The Hindu*, says: The low status of the barber profession in India goes way back. The Buddhist *Jataka Tales* (4th Century BC) narrate the story of a barber's son who falls in love with a girl from the high Licchavi clan. His father reminds him of their low social status and assures him, in vain, that he will help him find a bride from his 'own place and station' (in WHD Rouse's 1895 translation). The son dies longing for his love.

The word nai is a corrupt form of the Sanskrit word napika, or 'one who cleans nails'. Myth has it that the god Shiva

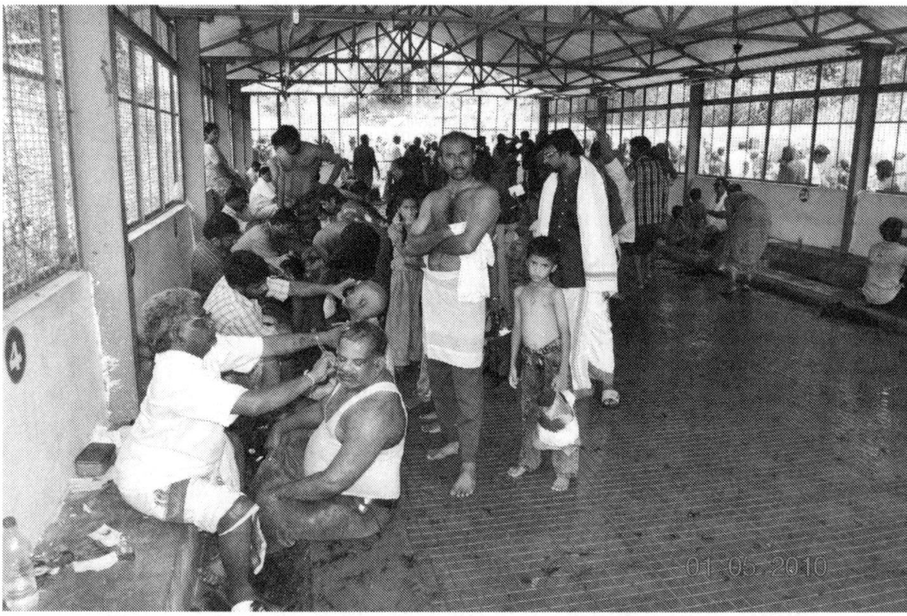

Thousands of devotees get their hair cut at the Tirupati Tirumala temple where hair is an offering

(god of destruction) created them from his navel to cut and clean the nails of his consort Paarvati. They are also said to be descended from a Kshatriya (warrior class) father and a Shudra (cultivator class) mother.

The *Upanaishads* (Jaiminiya Upanishad Brahmana and Chandoga Upanishad) mention a line of kings that include Abhipratarin, who is said to be the nephew of Janamejaya, the storyteller of the Mahabharata epics. According to historian HC Raychaudhuri (Political History of Ancient India), this line of rulers, known as the Saisunagas, also included the famous Buddhist king Bimbisara and his Hindu son Ajaatsatru. According to the *Puranas*, Mahapadma Nanda (c. 345 BCE), the founder of the Nanda dynasty was the son of the last Saisunaga king by a shudra woman (a low caste woman of the barber community) and father of Agrammes. Curtius, a Roman historian, informs us that: His (Mahapadma's) father was in fact a barber, scarcely staving off hunger by his daily earnings, but who, from his being not uncomely in person, had gained the affections of the queen, and was by her influence advanced to too near a place in the confidence of reigning monarch. Afterwards, however, he treacherously murdered his sovereign, and then, under the pretense of acting as guardian to the royal children, usurped the supreme authority, and having put the young princes to death begot the present king (Mahapadma Nanda). According to Jain texts, Mahapadma was the son of a courtesan and a barber, who with the help of his barber father and the queen of the last king, usurped the kingdom. The last of this line was Agrammes of the classical texts. The Nandas, under Mahapadma Nanda, established the first great North Indian empire with its political centre in Magadha. His kingdom annexed parts of Kalinga, central India, Anga, and the upper Ganges valley. He was the first shudra king of *Magadh* and it was his consolidation that led to the famous Gupta empire several centuries later.

In the Arabic tradition, it is said that God first ordered Archangel Gabriel to shave Adam. Thus Adam learnt the art of shaving and handed down the art to Sulemain Paras, or the Prophet Solomon. The community claims descent from the Prophet Solomon or Sulaiman, and often call themselves Salmani. They maintain a manual of their art, known as the *Kisbatnama*. The word hajaam is derived from the Urdu word 'hajaam (barber)', itself coming from the Arabic word hijama. This word can easily acquire shades of ridicule. It is not uncommon to abuse someone as a hajjam or to say, 'Am I doing hajjamat here?' to assert that one's work is not inconsequential. In most parts of India, hair work continues to be socially devalued.

Rulers like Mahmud of Ghazni and Mohamed bin Tughlaq are known to have recruited from among Muslim converts from the barber castes for high positions in the army and administration. In India, the status of barbers has been low among Indian Muslims also as much of the community are converts from Hindu low castes. Historically, they have been concentrated in the Awadh region, but are found throughout North India, Sindh and united Punjab area. Jalalabad, Habib Ahmed's ancestral village in UP, is part of the Afghan settlements in the region who came with all the conquistadores from the North.

The barber also forms a part of popular literature in the subcontinent, stories galore of Birbal (The Wicked Barber's Plight) and the barber who wanted to send Akbar's minister 'to heaven', and Tenali Raman in the South of India. Krishnadevaraya, the king of Vijayanagar, had a barber who gave the king a fine shave while he was asleep (and spared him the discomfort that came with a shave back then). Delighted with the shave, the king granted the barber a wish. The Barber asked to be made a 'Brahman'. The king summoned his Brahmin priests and asked them to confer a Brahman's status on the barber and promised, in return, to exempt them from taxes. Unaware of rituals for enabling the barber's wish, they approached the wise Tenali Raman, the court jester for help. Tenali Raman asked a few of them to assemble on a riverbank with the paraphernalia for ritual conversion. He brought a black dog to the riverbank, bathed it and walked it around the ritual site. When Krishnadevaraya asked Tenali to explain this bizarre ritual, the jester replied that he was trying to turn the black dog into a white one. The jester argued that if a barber could become a Brahmin, then the dog's coat could as easily be changed.

Tenali Raman with barber in the barber-Appu series

Chandan Gowda writes: In an essay on the meanings of hair in the sub-continent, Patrick Olivelle, the Sanskritist, observes that discussions in ritual literature have consistently held hair as an impure object. This is a probable reason for hair-related service occupation to invite low social status. The fact that barbers also performed minor surgeries and played musical instruments did little to alter their status.

The traditional nai, Hindu or Muslim, groom clients by cutting hair, nails and circumcising and provide minor medical services like extracting teeth and setting sprains right. They also perform duties in connection with marriage, matchmaking and celebrations. Nai women, called 'Naun', are hairdressers, henna artists and midwives. Yet they are 'untouchables' even in the 21st century.

'Untouchability brings another facet to the social experience of humiliation. The village barbers usually serve upper castes and Dalits with separate sets of instruments. Recently, in a village in Tumkur in Karnataka, the barbers refused to serve Dalits, forcing the latter to learn to cut their own hair', Gowda writes.

Though they interact closely with all other communities, and despite a patron-client relationship, they are still regarded as a low caste community due to their occupation. Higher castes generally do not accept food and water from the hands of the nai and they in turn do not accept the same from some lower castes such as the Chamar (tanner), Balmiki (sweeper), Mochi (cobbler) and Bazigar (acrobat).

Nais are part of the shudra caste. Shudra were artisans and craftsmen—woodworkers, gardeners, herders, laundresses, potters and barbers. The Shudra caste was just above the Harijan caste, the 'Untouchables', but was lower than all other castes. One expert says, 'All people in the Shudra castes were regarded as inferior to upper castes, because of their impurity. Impurity came from contact with "polluting" substances and social situations. The lowest caste, the Harijan, came in contact with the dead, pigs and excrement. Among the Shudra, the Mirasis, singers, were superior to henna artists. Singers could entertain upper castes and were exposed to their gaze, but they didn't have to touch them. Nais touched hair, feet and blood and thus were more polluted than singers.'

THE PHILOSOPHY

Writing about a hair stylist, a thought came into my mind—is there a 'philosophy' behind hair and hair styling? This term 'philosophy of hair' seems funny but I think that every action has its own theory. Then why not hair and all that is done with it? From this curiosity, I started a search on the internet and I found some questions. It seems to me the following are recognisably philosophical questions:

What distinguishes a haircut from other events in which one's hair ends up shorter? Is a good haircut timelessly good, or does the quality of a haircut depend in part on the tides of fashion? Must a haircut please its bearer to be good? Are there, perhaps, several different dimensions of 'goodness' to be pulled apart here? To what extent should a haircut be judged by the intent of the hairdresser? These questions created an urge to find answers and who is better than Habib Ahmed to answer?

Now, maybe these aren't earthshakingly important philosophical questions but they do bring forth the issue of aesthetics. Habib Ahmed asks, 'Why do I care whether there is a philosophy of hair? Here's why. If there is, it suggests that philosophy is not just a subject area. It is an approach, a style of thinking, a willingness to plunge in and consider the deepest ontological, normative, conceptual, and broadly theoretical questions regarding anything.'

But for me the basic question has been how anyone's personality is deeply associated with a hair style? In an article written by Sean Gittins in 2013 in the magazine *Philosophy*, he says that 'The links between a philosopher's ideas and the hairstyle he or she chose to adopt were also demonstrated by the great religious philosophers. St Augustine of Hippo, before his conversion to Catholicism, sported long greasy locks much like we would today associate with a Hell's Angel or a Goth. Refusing to wash his hair, it became unruly and dreadlocked. It was not until Augustine had a personal message from God that he altered his unfashionable and unholy ways. He recollects the moment he was convinced of Catholicism in his autobiography, *The Confessions.* He says: 'I heard a song that told me to read the book of the Lord, which I would, findeth much goodness therein, and that for Pete's sake

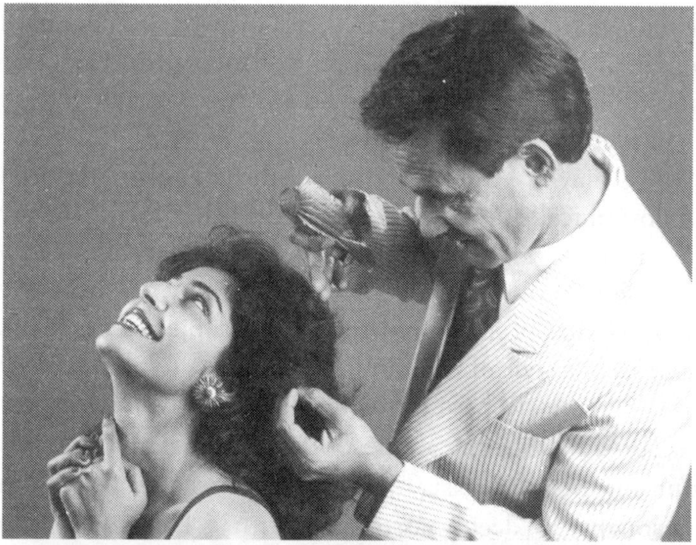

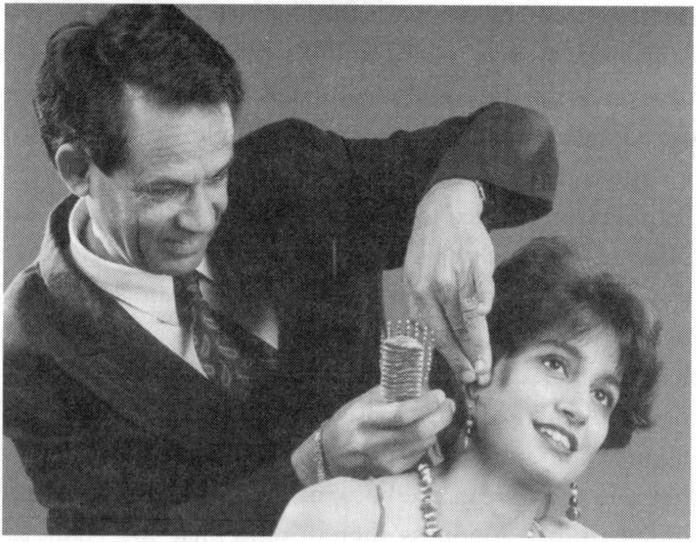

I should cutteth mine terrible mane of haireth!' Persuaded by this message, he cut his hair in accordance with Holy Orders, believing the 'hairy ring' style to be purer and more religious. He never regretted the decision, saying that his hair was much easier to manage at so short a length. To gain maximum precision, he cut his tonsure around his head using a compass. He was severely teased for this by other monks, who nicknamed him 'Pristine Augustine'. Augustine began to preach the benefits of a Christian way of life, particularly the hair, to the people of Hippo.

They were not convinced, and when he died the majority of Hippo's population still sported afros.' This is amazing to read, because in day-to-day life, one hardly thinks of topics like that. I am not speaking here of the time to think but the key is awareness. Habib too strongly emphasis this. One must know how the world thinks in order to be a good stylist. 'As the twentieth century dawned, so too did a new philosophy of hairstyles. The groundbreaking work in logic and the philosophy of language of Frege, Russell, and the young Wittgenstein, was accompanied by neat and logical side-partings. However, Wittgenstein renounced his earlier haircut when he renounced his early philosophy, changing his parting from the left to the right side of his head to illustrate the severity of the intellectual break. Russell told him he was mad for doing this, and the two fell out soon after. Despite his failure to find the foundations of hair, Russell never abandoned his own side-parting. He always believed the reason he won the Nobel Prize for Literature in 1950 was because of his slick cut rather than his writing.' In India too, there is a surge of awareness which has resulted in legal remidies, if not fashion or style sanctions. In 2011, before stepping down as Chief Minister of Karnataka, BS Yeddyurappa had promised to issue an order prohibiting the use of the word hajjam. He was addressing the members of the Karnataka Savitha Samaja, an association of traditional barber castes. (According to myth, Savitha was a sage who used to cut the hair of gods.) Such a prohibition aims to make illegitimate, and probably punishable too, the use of a term laden with memories of humiliation and restore respect to hair work. Whether banning words makes their meanings more potent and gives them a secret lease of life is another discussion. In 2009, the Salon and Beauty Parlours Association (SBPA) in Maharashtra protested against the term 'barber' in the title of the Shah Rukh Khan starrer, *Billu Barber*. The protestors pointed out that 'barber' was a translation of nai, a Hindi word for the barber caste, and, therefore, amounted to an insult. The President of the SBPA asked that the film's title be changed to Billu Hairdresser since the word barber was a derogatory and insulting term. He noted further: We choose hairdressing as a profession because it is an art. Also there are many women hairstylists. They said, 'If Billu Barber becomes a hit, women hairdressers will be called barbers too!'(Admitting innocence, Shah Rukh Khan agreed to have a white paper pasted over the offending word in the film posters as reprinting them was expensive.)

EMPOWERING THE OTHER

When Nazir Ahmed's scissors touched a person's hair, it was like poetry being written and it was completely unconsciously that Habib was pulled towards this art form. Nazir was a barber of high stature at that time. He was the President's barber, no less. But Habib was always acutely aware that his father was just a nai. It is not a respectful job even today, roadside barbers are considered of very low status in society. In the 1950s, Rs 150 was not enough for a 11-member family. Nazir earned just 150 rupees a month even as the President's barber and Habib is the eldest of nine children. Habib had no option at that time and he had to go to work at the age of 15 to help his family. In all these days of struggle a word always haunted Habib, 'nai' or 'hajjam'. Young Habib hated the word nai (barber). That was the reason why he had never wanted to join his father's profession.

Habib wanted to be a professional footballer. Then how's a childhood without passion? 'I was playing very good football in those days. At that time, football had a big place in the Indian heart and we had a very strong atmosphere of football in the Rashtrapati Bhavan. My biggest dream was to become a football player. There were a number of teams, so the only reputed pass to enter a team was to enter the Railways and get included in the Railways team. To remain in the game, I decided to be an engine driver to get into the Railways Football Team', Habib confides. Exactly like India's cricket captain Mahinder Singh Dhoni's story of trying to remain in cricket in the 2000s. Only Habib Ahmed came fifty years before. In India, then as now, games were not thought of as professions.

Habib's physic was athletic and he played football for the President's Estate team. He was one of the brightest players of his time in the Rajaji Football Tournament. But Habib's destiny lay elsewhere.

The skill of 'haircraft' was there somewhere inside Habib. Just like in his son Jawed, who studied French but finally took up his father's vocation. Habib's childhood friend Zameer says, 'we couldn't imagine that one could go so high in a career like nai. Today hairstyling is a respected profession, but not long ago people looked down upon this occupation. Habib Ahmed is a key person behind this change of perception'.

In a television interview, Habib was asked a question on how he perceived India after practicing his vocation here for so many years. His answer, 'I see this question through my professional journey. India is on a path of development and now being at par with the rest of the world is not very far away. There is a new wave of thinking and exposer to modern societies across the world. People now recognise my work respectfully, that was not the case earlier.'

Gone are the days of Birbal and Tenali Raman and the status of the nai of those times, an odd-jobs person and jack of all trades, lending an ear to the king and the courtesan, keeper of secrets that make or break empires; nevertheless ostracised by society, untrustworthy, untouchable and often unkempt as in Chekov's story.

In spite of the community backdrop and its accompanying hurdles, Habib Ahmed has in a single generation managed to radically change the image of the nai to that of a suave stylist, flamboyant in his craftsmanship, astute in his business acumen and generous in his dealings with society. Today's nai stories are therefore very different from the tales of yore.

> In June 2003, a girl came to meet Habib Ahmed through an NGO. Her name was Sunaina. She had lost her family in Saharanpur of Uttar Pradesh during a clash between two communities. (Name, place changed.) She was a victim of polio and unable to walk properly, somehow she manage to carry herself with the help of calipers.
>
> Sunaina was fifteen-sixteen years old and did not know what to do with her life. She had lost all hope of a future following the communal clashes. Habib readily took her into his hairstyling academy. She was an introvert by nature but very conscious and alert in her learning. After four weeks of training at Habibs, she became an expert stylist. When it was time for her to leave, Habib saab asked her, 'what are you going to do now, after this workshop?'

> Sunaina paused, then wiped her eyes and replied, 'people often called me langri, but now, when I got an opportunity to join this workshop and get training from a person like you, people admire me and nobody now calls me a langri.'

'These were inspirational words for me', says Habib senior. 'A skills set can change a person's life and that I have the wherewithal to impart this skill makes me feel all-powerful', Habib says remembering that moment. 'I felt so empowered—that I can not only change one's hair style but I have the ability to change someone's personality and people's perspectives.'

Some people are very impatient on the subject of religion and they make noises everywhere on this issue, says Habib Ahmed, on retrospection. What does matter is what you can do—even a little something—for any needy person, irrespective of his/her religion. 'This is the biggest religion, to help or show someone the right path, this matter a lot.'

Habib saab can be an example of charity. A model of charity through skill development. An apt ambassador for the Prime Minister's Skill India campaign. For the last two decades Habib and his sons have all been deeply associated with several non-government and social organisations, and these organisations all call the Habibs to conduct or participate in hairstyling workshops, as career guides and mentors. Habib saab emphasise that he wants to share his skills with others in order to empower them. He wants to contribute more than he is doing now. 'This is not for the sake of any "*Jannat*", but this is for my satisfaction. This skill I can share and it should be shared', says Habib saab.

Surender is getting late for his shift in a saloon in Delhi. After ten minutes of searching, finally he finds an auto rikshaw. It will take 30 minutes form Laxmi Nagar to Connaught place, where his work place is situated. Surender spent five years in this famous saloon as a specialised long hair stylist. Today he had to go to his daughter's school to pay the monthly fee, and he is late for work. But he knows that his manager will excuse him for the day.

Surender remember the magic line Habib Ahmed told him five years ago. 'Always stand on your present and think about your future.' These line changed his life forever. On that day, Surender was wandering in the streets of east Delhi. He did not know exactly how he came to Delhi form Bareli (Uttar Pradesh). He was a teenager then. In 1997, he was picked up by an NGO, Amar Jyoti, and went through the process of rehabilitation.

'Someone sent me to them. My parents were not with me, I was alone. The big question before me was where I should go? What am I going to do for the rest of my life? The NGO sent me to train at Habibs. In those tough days, Habib Saab assured me that he will take care of me.' Gradually, Habib started teaching Surender all about hair styling. 'To match his stamina and concentration was tough. Moreover, Habibji is very disciplined and a strict teacher, he was not ready to forgive even the slightest negligence. Many times he scolded me. Often this made me angry. But even then, I knew that probably all these strictures were only for my betterment, and I was right', recalls a grateful Surender.

It was 26 November night in 2008. The port city of Mumbai was under terrorist attack and the nation was watching the carnage on television.

Gajender Singh was a member of the National Security Guard's 51 Special Action Group. Singh was part of the team of NSG commandos who were on the roof of Nariman House in an operation to neutralise the terrorists inside who were holding at least six hostages. Singh then lead one of the teams that entered the building. The team came under intense fire from the terrorists and returned fire, while trying to dominate the situation. The terrorists also hurled a few grenades at the commandos. At this point, Singh had the option of retreating with his team. However, he realised that they had to seize this opportunity to dominate and continued moving ahead. He didn't turn his back to the militants and created a way for the other commandos though a grenade was thrown at him. Despite sustaining multiple bullet injuries while doing so, he moved forward and ultimately succumbed to his injuries, making the supreme sacrifice. His act of bravery was honoured with the Ashoka Chakra.

In this background of supreme sacrifices, what can a common man do? We can praise the hero, build memorials and name a road after him. But a Hero who sacrifices his life for his country also has a family and very few of us remember this. On 5 December 2008, Habib Ahmed decided that he would keep open his shop all night. The all-night service managed to generate Rs 100,000 for the commando Gajender's family. Habib Ahmed felt that the best way to help in such a situation was to use his particular kind of art to generate financial aid, and express solidarity with the braveheart's family.

IN TIHAR JAIL

Who? Habib?

What's a hairstylist doing in a jail?

Believe it or not, a hairstylist can be a turning point in many lives. Such a person, s/he is not only related to your looks but can be related to your life itself. Yes, Habib Ahmed today is not only an exalted nai, he is a lifeline giver to inmates of Asia's biggest jail, the Tihar Jail. A reformist of sorts.

Having a hair cut at an upmarket Habibs' saloon at a cost of Rs 560-Rs 1,100 could be your idea of comfort but inmates at Tihar Jail are now able to afford the luxury—almost. Bollywood movies still love to show the inmates of a jail as those being made to crush stones all the time, but the reality is something else altogether. The high-end hair and beauty parlours in the prisons now select and train Tihar prisoners in modern hair styling.

Each of the 10 prisons in Tihar once upon a time had a government barber who offered services free of cost. In addition, a few prisoners also doubled up as barbers. At any

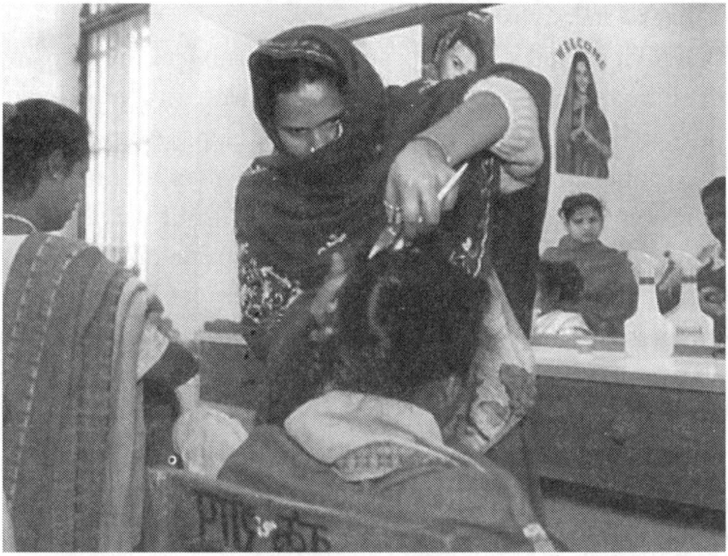

Delhi's Chief Minister Sheila Dixit inaugurated the Tihar jail prison saloon where the Habibs first trained the stylists in the women's prison as a part of their vocational training and later trained the male prisoners to become professionals and start new lives as hairdressers

point of time, there would be 10 barbers for every 1,500 prisoners. Apart from these barbers, other willing inmates would also be allowed to take training. On a cold January morning in 2008 Habib senior decided the jail barbers needed to improve their services. He and his son Amjad devised a plan. 'I will hold a seminar in the jail and hope to begin the first batch with women prisoners, who will, in turn, train others', Amjad told his father.

Tihar officials were delighted with the Habibs plan. This would add to the various vocational activities already in place for imparting professional training to inmates, who can begin lives afresh with new skills once released from the jail. The traditional jail barber rooms have been equipped with the latest equipment and tastefully redone. Habibs now use dummies on which trainee prisoners learn their skills. At first, they taught prisoners hair cutting, facial and makeup, now some get more advanced training. Amjad is the one who today manages the Tihar training facility for hairdressing. Habib Ahmed proudly says, 'Such activities motivate prisoners to lead a normal life and also equip them professionally to earn a respectful living.'

THINKING DIFFERENTLY

'In 2009, Habibs also began a hairstyling training course for sex workers', Amjad Habib tells us. However, this turned out to be a greater challenge than the jail. GB Road is Delhi's notorious red light district and not only social

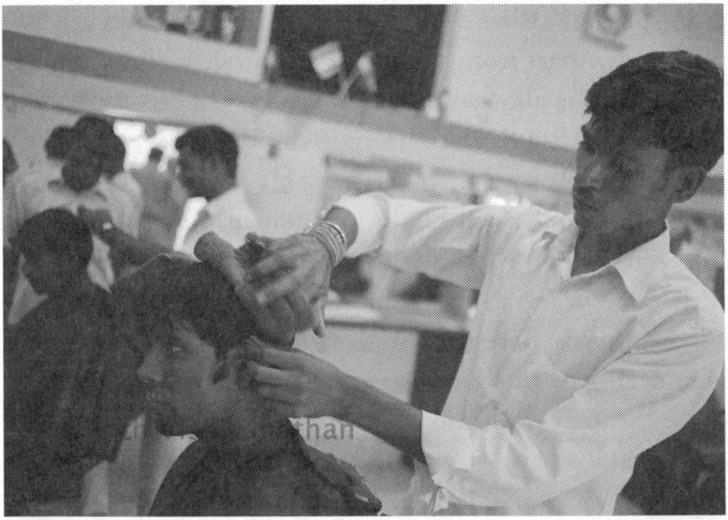

Tihar jail prisoners demonstrating their skills

workers but everyone including health workers will agree skill-training (as beauticians, hairdressers, cooks, drivers etc) for the women here would help tremendously in reestablishing their dignity, and alternative employment can bring tremendous social change in the community.

Of course, there are vested interests who always want a status quo and sex work is one of the world's biggest money churning industry today. Habibs' farsightedness was, naturally, vehemently opposed by pimps and middlemen exploiting the women and the low confidence and education level of these women themselves resulted in the first initiative being withdrawn within a few weeks, after several attempts to convince the community failed. The Habibs have not given up the idea though. They know they are right. If the HIV awareness initiative has succeeded all across India and the transgender community has been persuaded to consider alternative employement, the Habib family think, very soon their effort with sex workers will see a new life again. 'We will start this again soon', an optimistic Habib senior says.

On the eve of Children's Day 2002, the house of Habibs and Child Relief and You (CRY) launched a chair of 'Thousand Smiles' programme for underprivileged children. Under this programme, the customers at the Haibib saloons in DLF, Gurgaon, Punjabi Bagh and South Extension get a chance to gift a smile to a needy child by having a hair cut with 20 % of the proceeds going to CRY. The Habib Hair Academy also provides a three-

Classes in progress in Habib academies

> months free hairstyle course to 12 best CRY students (7 girls and 5 boys). 'This specialised course equips them to face the job market with greater confidence and earn a decent livelihood. It's better to impart technical education rather than give money', says Jawed Habib. 'It was basically my father's Idea. He has taken up the responsibility of looking after the education part.'

It was January 1988. In the morning around 11 o'clock Habib got a call from a nongovernmental welfare organisation called Amar Jyoti. By now he was a brand, and he knew he could make a difference even through a tiny start. After this phone call he sat on his couch and all his life stood in front of him as a slide show. Each slide described what a tough struggle he had. After almost one hour, he got up and decided that it was time for giving back.

'I feel satisfied if I do something for the needy. Earlier I was associated with Amar Jyoti where I trained underprivileged girls, the most vulnerable part of our society. I wish I could do it in a much bigger way', adds Habib Ahmed. 'The basic objective is to give a child an opportunity in life to break the vicious cycle of ignorance and poverty, and help flourish his/her full potential.'

Habib senior confesses, 'I have been running and running all my life. One thing I always had in my mind. Finally it was a window provided to me with the help of many others. Yes, my zeal was there to do something for social

A Habibs presentation in progress at a class on skill development

uplift but somebody had to stand by me and show the way. When this idea of training for these marginalised people came to my mind, definitely, my thinking about it also became a small window for others to grab at opportunity.' Habib senior is emphatic, 'I have to share what I know'. Sharing of knowledge is important, 'it improves your own creativity', he adds. He is not afraid that his students will ever compete with him. He confidently says with a smile, 'When these people reach where I am today, I'll be ahead by then. I'll welcome competition though.' This can only be said by a person who has not only reached the zenith of his achievements but by one who has gone beyond, become a community icon, a change-imparting society leader, a man who can give back to the country unstintingly. And to give back, one must have something to give. Habibs is not just a haircut, it is knowledge and skills they return in manyfolds.

London Dreams

As a barber to Lord Mountbatten (the first Governor-General of the independent Dominion of India, 1947-48), and then Prime Minister Jawaharlal Nehru, Nazir Ahmed was entitled to a residence within the campus: House No 32, Block No 12. This took his family into the shadows of the Rashtrapati Bhavan where all the support staff lived.

In the President's Estate, Nazir's quarters was a 150 sq feet room with one tap for water. At that time there were 52 such quarters in the Estate. Toilets were for common use. Nazir lived here with his wife and nine children. Some people here had the luxury of having a radio and a few had morning newspapers, but Nazir and his family were far from these sort of facilities.

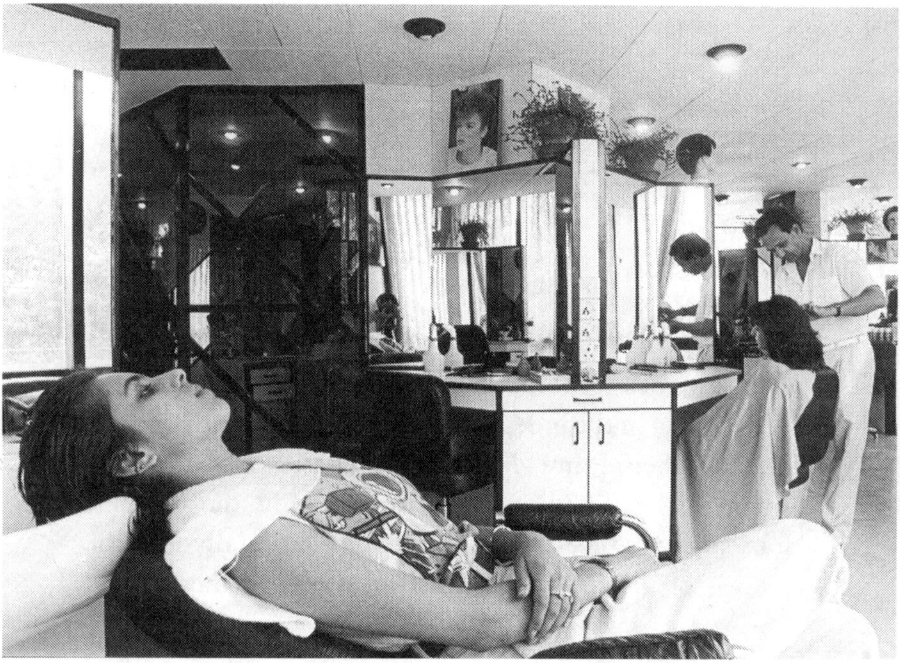

Habib Ahmed training at the Morris school

Lady Mountbatten would often come to see the living conditions of the support staff. On Eid and Diwali, bigwigs would come with sweets. Habib senior recalls that his father had a very comfortable life. 'He would go to give a haircut or shave and then the entire day he was with us. They led a non-materialistic life. I remember the entire compound had two radio sets and in the evening we used to sit together to listen to news and music.'

Habib's eyes dampen as he recalls the days of his childhood spent at the Rashtrapati Bhavan.

This building was majestic and luxurious, but Habib Ahmed always kept in mind that 'the other side of this majestic house was servant quarters. It was pathetic to live there. There was a difference in facilities among British and Indian employees. We were nine brothers and sisters and our parents. But we were only given one room and a small court yard. We had to use common bathroom and toilets. Yes we were like servants.'

Nazir always shared his experiences and thoughts and memories about the Viceroy's House, the British rule and his belief in India and the Indian people with little Habib. One of his anecdotes was that Mountbatten loved to apply oil in his hair and arrange his hair upwards; he often said, hair is like a crown over the head. Mountbatten was warm towards the staff serving him. 'I respect Lord Mountbatten not because he helped me to get to London but because of his great affection and humanity', Habib adds, saying Mountbatten was an exception.

After India got independence, Mountbatten asked Nazir Ahmed if he, too, was thinking of migrating to Pakistan. During the time of partition, Mountbatten gave Nazir a choice to stay in Pakistan, London or India. This was a dilemma but on the day of the decision, Nazir told Mountbatten, 'I don't want to go anywhere, be it Pakistan or London. I want to die for this country where my forefathers lived.' A proud Nazir told Mountbatten, 'I was born in India and I will die an Indian.'

Again, it was Lord Mountbatten who once asked Nazir Ahmed, 'Why don't you send your son to London?' With these magic words began Habib Ahmed's London dreams. Mountbatten knew that the young Habib wanted to go abroad and he was willing to help the young man. The question was, how would it be funded and what would he be doing there? Rajkumari Amrit Kaur suggested that Habib should have some experience in India before going to start professional training in London. At that time, Rajkumari Amrit Kaur used to go to Roy n' James in Connaught Place, Delhi. In that era, Roy n' James was a well-known hair saloon. It was run by Roy, a Punjabi businessman. With a recommendation from Amrit Kaur, Habib got a chance to work in Roy n' James.

Roy was quite impressed with this young man. He was a quick learner and enterprising. Roy learnt that Habib wanted to go to London for further training and he was supportive. Habib needed travel funds and expenses to get through in London for the first few months. This would be quite a large sum of money. His father had absolutely no money to support Habib.

Roy provided Habib part funding, the air ticket and 50 pounds but made the young man sign a contract that upon returning to India, Habib would work only for Roy. They told everyone that Habib's wife had sold her jewellery to fund his study. The story they floated was, naturally Habib wanted a better deal in life for his family of five sisters and two brothers, one of whom was a polio victim. Habib's father was by now 53 and still had a few more years to retire. This was the right time for Habib to go abroad. Habib's youngest brother would be old enough to succeed his father by the time Nazir retired, thus continuing the ties with the Rashtrapati Bhavan and with the elite of Delhi.

Asked about her marriage, Habib's wife Hashmi has told the media, 'We have been married for 50 years. We married when I was 18 and before he left for London.'

'Our first meeting was very filmi', says Habib. 'There was a wedding in the family and when the baraat came, there was a lot of excitement. We met on the narrow stairs leading up to the roof. She was running down and I was racing up the stairs. We both stopped at once. I couldn't get her out of my mind and when she sent me a note through a small boy, we met and I sent my father to her house. We were married soon after'. Hashmi had to bear with a lot of hardships and the initial years of the marriage were

Mountbatten helps barber Habib obtain London training course

By K. K. DUGGAL
Gemini News Service

NEW DELHI, India: The efforts of Earl Mountbatten — the last Viceroy of India — to help a young New Delhi barber succeed in his career have moved even the stony heart of the Reserve Bank of India.

Habib Ahmed is 27, a rising young hairdresser in the Indian capital. He tints, bleaches, waves and sets with the best.

He has trimmed President Zakir Husain's goatee, and given a short back-and-sides to the two sons of the Prime Minister, Mrs. Indira Gandhi.

But when he wanted to go to London for a six months' training course to improve his style, the Reserve Bank of India said "No." They refused to release the currency.

Nothing daunted, Habib approached Lord Mountbatten when the former Viceroy was visiting New Delhi last year.

After all, Habib's father Nazir trimmed Lord Mountbatten's hair when he was Viceroy — and the locks of Lord Wavell and Lord Linlithgow before him. And Nazir is still President Husain's personal barber.

Lord Mountbatten promised to do his best — and kept his promise. He wrote to the deputy prime minister and finance minister, Morarji Desai:

"When I was staying in Rashtrapati Bhavan (the Presidential Palace) in March the president's barber (who was with me as viceroy and governor-general) asked me to support the training of his son in England to be a really high-class ladies' hairdresser.

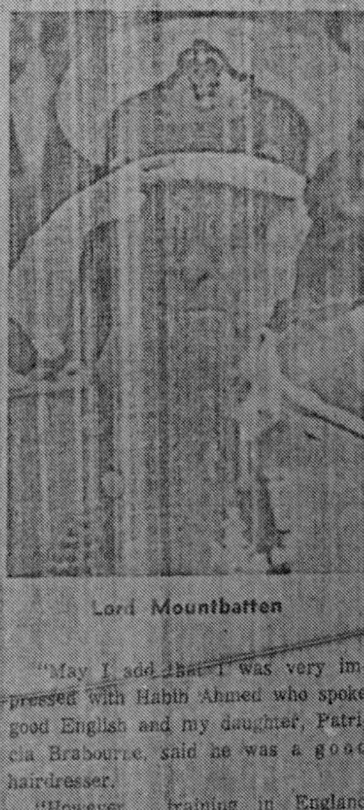

Lord Mountbatten

"May I add that I was very impressed with Habib Ahmed who spoke good English and my daughter, Patricia Brabourne, said he was a good hairdresser.

"However, training in England would make him fit for the highest class of hairdressing among the many ladies of your diplomatic colony and your high-class tourists, so I feel this would be a good thing for the prestige of Delhi."

Mr. Desai wrote back promptly:

"My dear Lord Mountbatten,

"I have received your letter, regarding training in the United Kingdom of the son of Nazir Ahmed. Normally, we do not encourage visits abroad on the basis of private sponsorship. However, in view of the very special interest you have shown in this case and the arrangements you have already made, the Reserve Bank of India are being advised to accord the requisite approval for the boy's training in the United Kingdom."

Later, Habib received a letter from the under-secretary of the finance ministry that "suitable instructions had been issued to the Reserve Bank."

His wife sold her jewels to help pay for the trip. Habib borrowed the rest from his employer, and he flies to London this week.

"My dream is coming true," he said. "Thanks to Lord Mountbatten."

Habib's father used to earn 150 rupees a month as the barber to viceroys and presidents. And Habib as the eldest of nine children, had to go to work at 15 to help support the family.

When he gets back from London he expects to be able to earn ten times his father's wage from the ladies of the diplomatic corps.

"First I'm going to pay off my debt, then I'm going to replace my wife's jewels," he said.

Habib's proudest memory — cutting the late Jawaharlal Nehru's hair five times. "He's always greeted me with 'How are you?' and at the finish would always say, 'thank you'."

very difficult. She worked in a tailoring unit producing sportswear for a company in Delhi's busy East of Kailash, to supplement the family income.

Soon after, Habib wanted to go to London. It was 1965. The total money needed for his stay and training in London was huge. Habib did not know where to stay in a foreign land, what sort of documents were needed for a visa and other travel formalities. Habib only had a letter from Lord Mountbatten, stating that his admission in the Morris Institute of Hair Dressing, London would be taken care of by Mountbatten. It was again Rajkumari Amrit Kaur, whose access in the corridors of power in Delhi were quite well known, who assured Habib that she would help him put his travel documents in place.

Habib was restless. London was calling him. He had Mountbatten's letter and was confident of success. The travel process was on. One technical step was the 'P' form. Taxes, super taxes and surtaxes had to be paid. At that time, however, Habib was clueless how everything would pan out to facilitate his London visit.

Lord Mountbatten wrote letters to Karan Singh (Prince of Jammu & Kashmir and a well known Congress leader) and also to the then union deputy prime minister and finance minister, Morarji Desai, asking them to help Habib. He wrote to Morarji Desai, 'When I was staying in Rashtrapati Bhavan in March, the President's barber asked me to support the training of his son in England to be a really

City barber wins London trip

H.T. Correspondent

New Delhi, March 27 — A city barber's resourcefulness has earned him a trip to London for advanced training in hair dressing.

The thorny path to London was cleared for Habib by no less a person than Lord Mountbatten who recommended the 27-year-old barber's case to Deputy Prime Minister Desai. The barber got the green signal from the Reserve Bank which had earlier rejected his application.

Habib had approached Lord Mountbatten who was here last year. Lord Mountbatten had had his hair trimmed by Habib's father, Nasir, before independence. Nasir had also served Lord Wavell and Lord Linlithgow.

But the Reserve Bank's permission did not end Habib's difficulties. He had to sell his wife's jewellery to raise money for the trip. He also took a loan from his employer.

On his return, Habib expects to earn ten times his father's income of Rs 150 from Viceroys and Presidents.

high-class ladies hair dresser. May I add that I was very impressed with Habib Ahmed and my daughter Patricia Brabourne said that he is a good hair dresser.' Even so, Lord Mountbatten wondered whether Habib could be given the necessary official clearance. He, thus, added, 'Training in England would make him (Habib) fit for the higher class of hairdressing among many ladies of your diplomatic colony and your high class tourists. So I feel, this would be a good thing for the prestige of Delhi.'

After receiving the letter from Mountbatten, Desai acted swiftly and also replied to the former Viceroy with, 'My dear Lord Mountbatten, I have received your letter regarding the training in UK of the son of Nazir Ahmed. Normally we do not encourage visits abroad on the basis of private sponsorship. However, in the view of the very special interest you have shown in his case and the arrangement you have already made, the Reserve Bank of India are being advised to accord the requisite approval for the boy's training in UK.' Later Habib received a letter from an undersecretary of the finance ministry that 'suitable instructions had been issued to the Reserve Bank of India'. With the then finance minister's help, Habib got the 'P' form in order. And after some conversions the RBI gave him 8 pounds, just 8 pounds for his expenses in London.

Habib, in retrospection of how things worked out to his advantage, says, *'kudrat ko jo manzur hota hai, wo hi ho jata hai* (if the Almighty has decided something then it is bound to happen). (Ref: Earl Helps Barber Habib to Brush up, *Sunday Mirror* London, 24 March 1968.)

Soon the media sniffed out that the government was helping this young man to study abroad. It was not easy to handle the media in those days. They asked prying questions: Who is this Habib? Why were politicians and powerful ministers more than willing to help him? Habib tried to avoid the media as much as possible. Someone told him publicity could hamper his dreams. The English daily newspaper, *The Statesman* did a story describing him as a shining talent who was ready to explore new avenues of entreprise and some big names like Louise Mountbatten and Morarji Desai were supporting him.

The Statesman drew a lot of attention to Habib, raising many eyeballs and a question was asked in Parliament from the Opposition bench, by none other than Atal Bihari Vajpayee himself. The question was simple: Why was the government favouring one man, helping him to study abroad? This was an unusual situation and this article marked a big leap for Habib's personal profile and future career.

LIFE LESSONS

Finally, Habib was all set to go to London. It was 1967 by then. Now the media wrote: 'Habib is the eldest son of the President's barber. A bright-eyed scion of the family that took pride in having shaved many a VIP chin. But

Habib knows that even a son of the President's barber must work for his keep. And the hard-headed young man that is Habib has been always planning a future for himself.' The newspaper added, 'he is not an ordinary barber but a ladies hairdresser, someone with a stake and reputation in the world of haute coiffure. With passion so rare Habib has been working hard to perfect his art in the native setting, but his heart is set on a stint in British salons. He even learnt English and is now very fluent in the language.'
Though Habib had managed a ticket for London, he still didn't get a visa. Officials at the Delhi airport did allow him to board the flight as he promised that he had a return ticket to Delhi.

But the real drama began once Habib reached the London airport. Custom and immigration people at the airport wondered how this young man had come so far without a visa. Habib was quite confident as he had a letter with him, a letter written by none other than Lord Mountbatten himself. Habib presented that letter before the airport authorities, raising their confusion to a different level. An officer came forward and questioned him. The letter was written six months before, so what made him come to London now? It was an old letter and obviously Habib was too late. Habib had no answer. The airport authorities were in a flurry, trying to establish the authenticity of the letter written by Mountbatten.

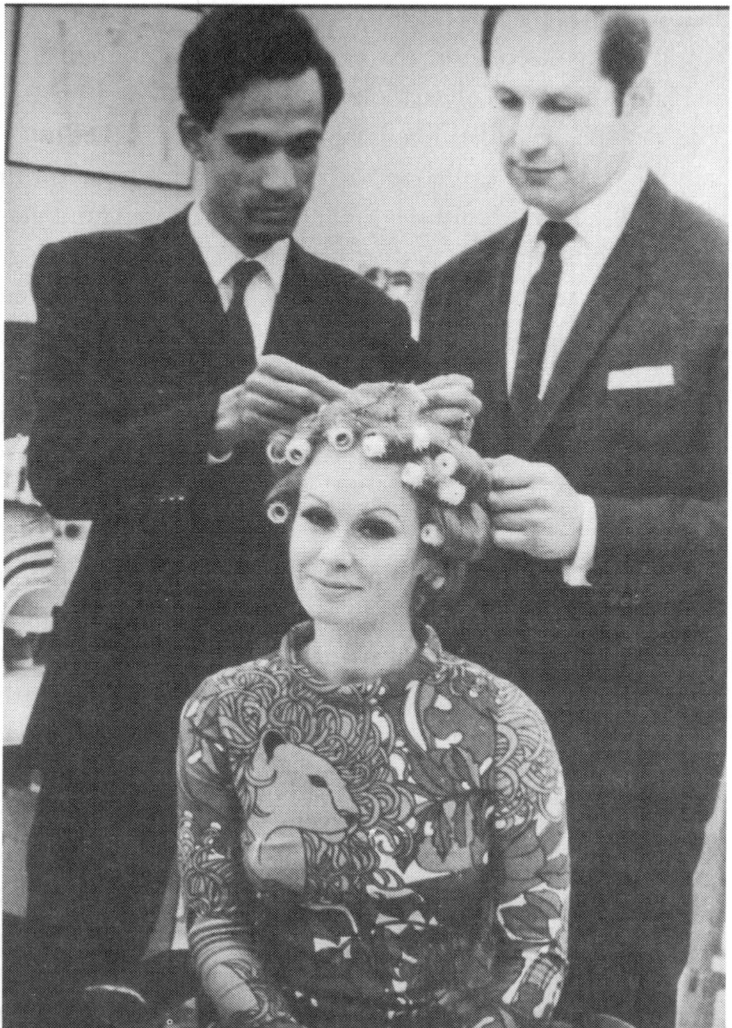

Habib Ahmed training in London

Habib tried to think, if he knew anyone in London. His employer, Roy in Delhi, had told Habib about Karim in London. Karim was his friend and there was some kind of a financial liaison between Roy and Karim. Roy had also insisted Habib meet Karim in London. So Habib came up with Karim's name. The British authorities called Karim. When Karim learnt about Habib, he sent a girl from his establishment to help Habib at the airport. For Habib it seemed like a never-ending wait at the airport, as he was rigorously drilled by various officers. Habib tried hard to communicate with them and explain his dreams but there was one more major problem, the language. However, despite his limited English, Habib managed to communicate with the officials—where he wanted to go, who he wanted to see.

Habib was hungry, for he had not been offered even a glass of water at the airport. After more than five long hours, British authorities issued him a visa for only two months. And the girl sent by Karim reached the airport and met Habib. After all the airport formalities were done this girl and her companions took him to a pub and asked him what he would like to drink. Habib simply told her that he did not drink and would appreciate if he could eat something. 'My dear you're far from the life', his escort told him. Then she ordered some sandwiches and Habib sighed in relief. Later on, she even arranged a room to stay for him.

He had crossed the seven seas. At last… Habib told himself London, the dream city of his fantasies, was so beautiful.

Habib with a batchmate in Morris School, London

Old buildings but clean and well maintained. Clean roads and smooth traffic. Most areas were full of greenery at that time. He was thrilled to experience the cold weather, historic buildings everywhere.

On day two Habib went and joined the Morris School in Piccadilly Circus. His admission was already through, thanks to Mountbatten. He then learnt that in his class of 20, he was the only man. 'I must say that initially I did not like the course at all. Earlier my thought was just to be in London, but when I reached London, I was blank. I wanted to play football. Now I think, how fortunate I was at that time. Though I had no "pounds" to meet my expenses, I had admission in the famous Morris School of Cosmetology. After a few days of initial hiccups, I managed to concentrate on my Cosmetology lessons. That was the first course. I never liked studying. I was slow in understanding what was being taught. There were three fat books on cosmetology to study, each for a different branch of the subject. I thought, I had got myself into a great mess.'

Habib was shy. The girls in his class laughed at his English. They laughed and made fun of the fact that a student of cosmetology applied mustard oil in his hair. They laughed at him because he wrapped his lunch in newspaper. Habib was aware of his financial status. However, slowly he became acclimatised to London's ways. The cultural shock was immense. The batch was full of diversity and included some Blacks, a few Asian and White students.

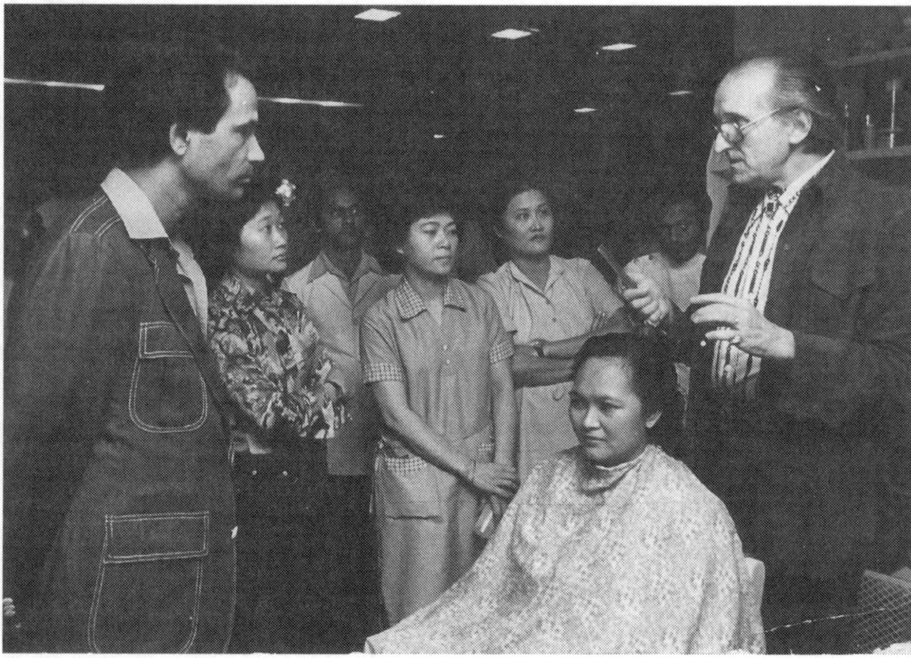

A class in progress at Mario's School

Habib remembers with a sparkle in his eyes how shocked he had been when a black girl and boy were kissing each other in the class room. He didn't know how to react. He was uneasy. Somewhere within himself he was missing something, he thought but what exactly was that… was it that he wasn't attracted to the opposite sex, or was he? He was in great dilemma.

Things changed, he became better and better in his lessons. 'Slowly, I came to terms with the English weather and temperament and by the fourth semester I was one of the most popular students not only amongst teachers but also with the girls', says Habib senior, recalling those pleasant memories. It was in the process of impressing girls that he acquired a taste for beer and dancing.

He lived in rented rooms at Leighton, often putting in a 16-hour day. Earlier, even the simplest house chores were done by his mother. Now they had become his responsibility. That was also when he worked out the philosophy of his life. He developed certain maturity and realised that it is not money but knowledge which is important.

Surviving in London is really tough if you don't have support. His 58 pounds were soon over. At that time travelling on the London metro cost 2.5 pounds for a month. So Habib walked from his home to and fro to the Morris School. This was physically exhausting. Initially, he lived on rice and milk for lunch and dinner as these were the cheapest food available. Then he had one meal a day, he

Habib with Mario

was a paying guest with a Punjabi family and generally had dinner at their table.

Someone suggested, he get a part-time job. But the rules of the institute prevented anyone from working even on a part-time basis. He managed to convince the principal, and he was finally given permission. Morris also got Habib a part-time job with Burton and Taylor as a salesman at the cash counter. He was paid 7.5 pounds per week. This saved Habib.

Habib was a trusted employee and he was placed in charge of the cash box. Soon, however, things began to go wrong. Two pounds were missing one day. And cashier Habib had no clue where the pounds went. He was very upset and did not want to be in charge of the cash box. However, his employer wanted him to do just that. When Habib requested to be assigned some other job, his employer, very upset, told him to wash dishes. That was what happened to Habib job-wise! At that point in time, Habib accepted what was offered to him, but realised that this could not continue for long. 'Is this the London that he had dreamt of, is this the London he had always wanted to come to and study, had knocked each and every door to reach here?', a desperate Habib thought.

Habib remembers these one-and-a-half years in London with a great deal of nostalgia. He had just four hours of sleep. Somehow he managed his classes, studies and the job. Besides juggling with all these, Habib had to also battle the cold. He was in no way equipped for London's winter. A friend from Pakistan arranged for a blanket and an overcoat for Habib. He was scared of taking a bath in cold water in this kind of weather. Habib did not have the best of outfits to wear those days but he says proudly, 'I had the cleanest clothes in class'.

'To become something big in life, one needs to sacrifice many things and the one who emerges a winner is the one who does not give in during difficult times', Habib says today. 'I love to visit London again and again', he says. He was fascinated by London and continues to be.

It was 1970. Habib had completed his course in London. He was tempted to continue to work in London. One day, Lord Mountbatten wanted to see him. When Habib walked in, he saw Prince Charles was also sitting with him. Habib was a bit nervous. His patron went straight to the point, asked Habib what his future plan was. Habib wanted to remain in London. Mountbatten said, no. Go back to your country, serve India.

Habib's classmate and people around him often asked him about India, but most of them had a pre-conceived notion about India. 'I was very disappointed with their views about India. They all though that India was a country with mosquitoes and flies... which meant... very dirty and backward.'

Though Habib thought about settling abroad, he had made a promise to Mountbatten. To come back to India to work. And he loved India. Despite the nostalgia, when he thinks of the British, Habib readily quotes Shashi Tharoor's speech in Oxford University on how the British only wanted to and exploited India. Tharoor reminds us, when Britain arrived on India's shores India's share of the world economy was 23 per cent, by the time the British left it was down to below 4 per cent. Britain's rise for 200 years was financed by its depredations in India. So Habib has no illusions about British rule in India or about Britain. Yet, he admits, England is the place for training and skill development in many fields, hairstyling being just one.

STRUGGLE FOR BREAD AND BUTTER

When Habib Ahmed came back to India, it was a very special moment, especially for his father. Habib had been away for long and far away. For Habib as well as his tradition-bound family, the journey had also been an internal voyage of discoveries, changes, mental adjustments, equality, respect, not just a matter of skill enhancement and Nazir Ahmed was speechless with joy. Nazir greeted his son but did not speak even a single word. Habib remembers that 'Abba didn't say anything but his eyes were full of love and ecstasy'. Nazir knew that this was the family's big moment of achievement; circumstances had been adverse, there was no money, just sheer willingness to achieve something and now it was done. Success loomed in the distant horizon.

On returning to India, Habib, contracted to Roy, joined Roy n' James as he had promised. There his work drew clients

Habib with Trevor Howard, an actor

and he became a very popular stylist. However, by 1971, the tension between India and Pakistan was tremendous and anti-Muslim feelings were at their height. Jealous colleagues began to use his religion as a ploy to get rid of him. 'When they threatened physical harm, Roy advised me to look for another job', says Habib. So, soon after returning to India, Habib Ahmed found himself jobless.

Moreover, Indian women didn't want to cut their hair.

He recalls that back then, mothers used to accompany young girls to prevent the barbers from sweet-talking their daughters into parting with their long tresses. 'I was taught, hair style depends on the geometrical proportion of the face but nobody was ready to hear me out. It took Indian women a long time to come out of this fascination for long hair. In fact, at one time I used to hate these Urdu poets who have written reams about the beauty of *zulfein** and compared it with thick clouds.'

From a historical point of view, Habib says, Indian women never experimented too much with their hair. 'The sculptures at Ajanta and Ellora prove it. The revolution came from the West which propagated that hair style is not something permanent and could be changed every few months. They came up with styles to sell their cosmetic products. When dyes went out of fashion, they introduced highlighting options....'

---

*Hair

So… Can you do long hair? This was the question that was asked to Habib Ahmed again and again when he entered the fledgling hairdressing industry fifty years ago. Having been set free by Roy, a jobless Habib went to a high-end parlour in Oberoi Hotel, Delhi. This was a well-known centre of hair dressing… where big names and socialites were clients. But here too Habib was again and again asked the same question, 'Can you do long hair?' Habib had no answer, he was clueless. After a long and detailed discussion, the managers of Oberoi decided to employ Habib but with a rider! Oberoi wanted to give him a chance, but told Habib that they would put him on probation for 15 days. During these 15 days Habib would have to prove to them that he could do any sort of hair. He was determined to fight all odds. He shivered in the nights and somehow just managed to earn his bread and butter. He was a qualified hair dresser from London and now here was he, forced to prove his skill! Habib was scared, didn't know what would happened to his dreams. But destiny had other plans for him.

Habib was young and, of course, studying abroad made him presentable. There was a beautician at Oberois at the time, a stylist called Elizabeth. Habib met Elizabeth who was charmed by him. Habib wasn't interested in her but he was tactful. He started learning how to do long hair from Elizabeth. The following months brought the two emotionally close too. Soon Elizabeth had a good offer to host a beauty pageant and she wanted to move out of the Oberois. Habib, however, declined to move from the Oberois. Habib started working sincerely and effectively. He had grasped the basics of styling of long hair and his work was appreciated so much that his long hair styles were displayed in Oberois' parlour window.

Many came to help him and Habib was on a mission to enhance or restructure his skill to find a foothold in this new scenario. He did extra shifts and long hours of work to prove himself. After 15 days, Habib was given full time employment in Oberoi, with a salary of Rs 750 per month. Now Habib was an expert in working on long hair, with the new Western hair style techniques. He made many friends and well wishers during his days in Oberois and in a very short time he built up a sizeable clientele too.

CREATING AWARENESS

In a country, where even today, the beauty or looks of a person are considered more important, it is indeed strange to find a person concentrate on hair. Habib justifies his obsession with hair as hair styling is for him more creative than the beauty side. 'There is a limit to what you can do with make-up, but not with hair. Your hair-style. It certainly improves your looks.'

'When I was younger, I would sink into terrible depression if even a single client was dissatisfied with my hairstyle', confides Habib. 'I often lost sleep over my one man's harsh words forgetting many satisfied customers I had during the rest of the day'. According to Habib, 'the profession acquired disrepute in India primarily because most of the people doing this job were from low castes. Abroad, things are different; the hair stylist is a part of the most exclusive strata of society. My attempt has always been to raise the standard of the art and to fill the vacuum in the Indian scene. In fact, in India we are still way behind the other nations as far as hair styling is concerned', Habib says.

'Hair styling is the most important personality trait', adds Habib, the Indian answer to Vidal Sassoon. It is important to frame the face with a suitable hairstyle, says he.
'The hands move through the long tresses with the ease bred of long familiarty, "hmmmm", good texture, good body, did you have a perm earlier? Get your hair massaged and washed, then I will give you your cut....
'The bemused girl, subject of master hairdresser Habib's attentions, submits meekly to the ministrations of an underling who gives her the soothing hair massage that is a Habib specialty, before setting her down for a thorough wash and shampoo. She is then led back to the master's presence, prepared like some sacrificial sheep for the ceremonial shearing', is how a writer described a hair cut at Habibs some years ago.
The description continues, 'a Habibs cloak is velcroid around her neck, the 52-year-old doyen of the scissor and comb fraternity settles her at the right angle into the padded chair and with the assistant passing him the appropriate set

of implements, gets down to perform with the dexterity of a master surgeon....

'Snip, Snip, Snip, Snip..the sound forms a soothing undercurrent as Habib cuts away, his voice soothing, with an explanatory murmur: "you have a full face, you see, so you need to emphasis your cheekbones, you need to let your hair fall back...." Handfull of shampoo soft hair, meanwhile, are twirled and pinned up, hefty chunks cut away altogether, snip, snip, snip... this is a normal day for Habib, but he knows how it was a gigantic task to convince a customer in early days....'

Even ten years ago, Habib points out, the words 'colouring', 'highlighting', 'mousse' and the like, drew blank looks. Beauty was considered more important than hair. 'Earlier, I used to get irritated a lot. But then I cooled down. It took a lot of patience and brain-washing to get to where I am today', he notes.

In an earlier recollection to the media, Habib says, 'Around 1974-75, an English hair stylist arrived. Everyone ran after him. No doubt he was very good, but you know how people are here, they always run after the foreigners.'

Habib remembers all the stories of that time, he says, 'that stylist was a blunt sort of chap, and I didn't talk much to him. But one day, I asked him what he thought of my work and he said, why should I work like a common hairdresser? I should became a stylist. He advised me to do a refresher course with Vidal Sassoon and so that's what I did. Sassoon is one of the top places in the world in this field and my experience of working with him set me thinking afresh. Abroad, I found that the stylists were very creative people and I also got the courage to be really creative, and not just technically competent.'

Men too have the urge to flaunt a winsome appearance. Shaping the hair into different styles is no longer a female prerogative as men have dropped inhibitions and frequent saloons to better their appearance.

The shag, the blunt, the wedge, the bald a la Sinéad O'Connor – from tousled to conservative to coy and to revealing your perfect shining pate – the crowning glory. Time to get out of the closet, hazard the bizarre and dare the hair. Fashion is not just restricted to wearing flamboyant clothes and accessories but extends towards having a trendy matching hairdo, keeping in tune with the changing times. What's in today could look dull tomorrow as change comes rapidly in this field. Hair styles can speak volumes about an individual's attitude, desires and personality. Where a blunt cut reflects a carefree and bubbly disposition, shag reflects a wild and carousal attitude.

Always there are whimpers of 'my!' and 'oh!' as locks of hair fall on the floor. Women abroad prefer a style that lets the fingers take over. Habib loves to style for the graceful Indian women. With his warm smile and caring touch, Habib has won many a head.

When he came back to India and gradually became well

known, many of his relatives asked Habib to change his name. Habib soon began to ask himself, 'Should I change my name?' The answer came from within. 'If I have seen a tough life, why should I hide the fact? After all, it has helped me in making me a stronger person'. The foreign-returned successful Habib was not ashamed of his name, that it represents a line of barbers. He actually was proud of his achievements and thought of it as a benchmark for his entire community. And with such strong views, Habib has worked tirelessly and hard to give dignity and status to the profession of a hair dresser.

RECOGNITION

'There is bound to be difference in a Paris designer outfit and one by a local tailor' Habib says, explaining that this holds true as well for hair. It is essential for a stylist to be well qualified. A person who lacks training can play havoc with his own reputation and the health of the client's hair. 'I find that people take such care of their health, they run to specialist doctors all the time, but they don't bother to get themselves a good hairdresser.'

WHAT IS BEAUTY?

In discussions about concept of beauty, Habib raises a few pertinent questions. These questions are directly related with skin colour and the 'Race' or racism issue. Habib says, 'We can divide this world in four colours. Actually this is not fair, but people do divide people in this manner. I don't believe in this. We see Black people in Africa and surrounding areas, people are White people in Europe, we Asian fall in the category of Brown and people like the Chinese and Japanese fall in to Yellow category. But the real problem is not with the colour. It is the mindset associated with the colours.' In an article titled 'Race without Color' written by Jared Diamond, Diamond strongly establishes this fact that 'Basing race on body chemistry makes no more sense than basing race on appearance—but at least you get to move the membership around.' Habib also emphasises that science often contradicts simple common sense. Our eyes tell us that the Earth is flat, that the sun revolves around the Earth, and that we humans are not animals. But science tells us otherwise.

With Habib senior, the discussion on race and colour moves further. 'The commonsense view of races goes somewhat like this: All native Swedes differ from all native Nigerians in appearance. There is no Swede whom you would mistake for a Nigerian, and vice versa. Swedes have lighter skin than Nigerians do. They also generally have blond or light brown hair, while Nigerians have very dark hair. Nigerians usually have more tightly coiled hair than Swedes do, dark eyes as opposed to eyes that are blue or gray, and fuller lips and broader noses. In addition, other Europeans look much more like Swedes than like Nigerians, while other peoples of sub-Saharan Africa—except perhaps the Khoisan peoples of southern Africa—look much more like Nigerians than like Swedes. Yes, skin colour does get darker in Europe toward the Mediterranean, but it is still lighter than the skin of sub-Saharan Africans. In Europe, very dark or curly hair becomes more common outside Scandinavia, but European hair is still not as tightly coiled as in Africa. Since it is easy then to distinguish almost any native European from any native sub-Saharan African, we recognise Europeans and sub-Saharan Africans as distinct races, which we name for their skin colours: whites and blacks, respectively. 'One should accept the creation of nature, but it should be above any petty identification of inferiority and superiority', Habib says.

You may think, what could be more objective? Research shows that this seemingly unassailable reasoning is not objective. There are many different, equally valid procedures for defining races, and those different procedures yield very different classifications, especially genetic mapping. One such procedure groups Italians and Greeks with most African blacks. It classifies Xhosas—the South African black group to which President Nelson Mandela belongs—with Swedes rather than Nigerians. Another equally valid procedure places Swedes with Fulani (a Nigerian black group) and not with Italians, who are again grouped with most other African blacks. Still another procedure keeps Swedes and Italians separate from all African blacks but throws the Swedes and Italians into the same race as New

Guineans and American Indians. Faced with such differing classifications, many anthropologists today conclude that one cannot recognise any human races at all. 'I find this issue very enlightening and the concept of beauty and mindset play their roles in tandem. The question is, whether issue of colour can and should be associated with beauty and fashion or smartness and if and when colour brings with it the feeling of inferiority for someone and superiority for someone else. I must say this is a burning question even today', says Habib senior, giving an example.

'When I was in London for my studies, there were two girls in our school from Kenya. These girls had a scratch mark on their forehead. I asked them how they had got these marks as these did not appear to be birth marks. They told me that, "in our country, this mark is considered as a symbol of beauty. We are proud to have this."' Coming from India, where skin colour has been the only criterion for thousands of years, for Habib it was an eye opener. For the first time he realised that the meaning of beauty varied in different parts of the world and what the real meaning of beauty is. He says that until and unless you are familiar with the many concepts of beauty, you cannot be a stylist. He quotes an article form *Huffington Post* blog, which says, 'Beauty has varied throughout time, various cultures and the vast different perceptions of the world. Beauty has been described and depicted through pictures and concepts penetrating our minds. Beauty has been defined in so many ways. What I have discovered is that beauty is simple. Beauty is happiness.

'It is the images and moments that inspire and represent the most distinct and remarkable attractiveness of our souls. It's the moments we feel free and real. It's the moments we feel proud and eminent. It's the moments we feel alive. It seems like that element should be inherent, but it isn't.

'Beauty is often distorted, misunderstood and shadowed by a wide amount of conflicting pressures. It is something we endlessly strive for, rather than see in the true essence of our happiest moments.'

Habib is angry that 'people don't care about their bodies… they are completely oblivious to what is going on inside their bodies. These people just come and say "make me trendy and beautiful", but it is not simple like that.' One should get the whole picture and not in pieces. One should be convinced that definition of beauty varies from person to person because everyone has a unique feature, complexion and body structure. One should not compare with anyone else and focus has to be on total health, the complete look.

'Inner strength brings real beauty. This concept is directly related with my profession of hair styling because we can only style better with good quality hair. So we have also started working on the overall quality of hair and improving it, not only focus on styling. Now our styling is a part of the total hair grooming', Habib senior explains.

'Everywhere, everybody wants to look better. First we

have to understand the concept of beauty, what is beauty', Habib goes on to add. Many people in this world have their own definition of what beauty is. 'Beauty can come from inside or the outside. We think that beauty comes from magazines or video girls or even models. I feel that I am beautiful because I have a great personality and I like to have fun. What beauty is not can be seen in the Barbie Dolls by Marge Piercy.'

'Beauty is a quality that pleases or delights the senses or mind. I think that beauty is all in what a person sees in another person. People see beauty as having blonde hair and exaggeratedly large breasts, tiny waists and curved buttocks. This is seen as the perfect image of what a women is suppose to look', says Habib, pointing out, 'this is not the complete truth and we should look beyond this typical thinking. One can be fair, brown or dark-black in their complexion, one may have sharp feature, sleek nose or broad face, heavy face with broad nose—these are not under a person's control.'

THE TEACHER

Parvez, Habib Ahmed's second son, has been a noted stylist for two decades now and is to be seen most often in the Habibs' main saloon. There is a famous saying that if you can't respect someone then you can't learn from that person. Respect is an essential requirement for learning from anyone. 'Even today, when Dad comes over to the shop, I can't work very well. I think it's out of *adab* (respect). I am the biggest fan of my father. I always tell my folks, when a rich businessman dies, nobody remembers him outside his corporate circle. But an artiste, even after his death, lives on through his work, his creations', says Parvez.

'My Dad's a great artiste. I feel he shouldn't work anymore. He has earned enough, struggled enough. He should now impart his knowledge free, something like what the Parisian hair stylist Alexandre does. Who knows, in ten years we could produce our very own Vidal Sassoon or another Alexandre. I want to teach whatever I know to others. I want Dad's magical words *"aaye buriya, jaye guriya"* to touch as many lives as possible', Parvez confides.

Everyone knows that observation is one of the most powerful tools to train one's self, and that is why Parvez says, 'Maybe I am more qualified than my father, but I want to learn everything he knows. But he always says, learn from experience. I keep telling him that before he dies he must teach me everything so that I can pass it on to my children. As a child I craved for my father's time. Even 20 minutes of it'. He does it even now.

The Rich and the Beautiful

Muntazir hun ki sitaron ki zara aankh lage,
Chand ko chhat par bula lunga eshara karke.

I am waiting for stars to sleep; I'll call the moon on the terrace. 'Sher o Shayari gives me pleasure and a sense of enjoyment of the things which are around me. Sometime we may not need to read more between the lines, just enjoy all that is around us', says Habib Ahmed.

Any form of art has only beautiful colours and attractive shapes, until and unless it has a thought behind the creation. The philosophy makes an artist a legend and thinking out of the box makes him/her a pioneer.

Habib's show was a show with a difference. For once, neither the models not their clothes were on display; instead emphasis was on their crowning glory, coiffeurs.

Statues at Ellora caves showing hairstyles popular from 6th centure BC to 6th Century AD

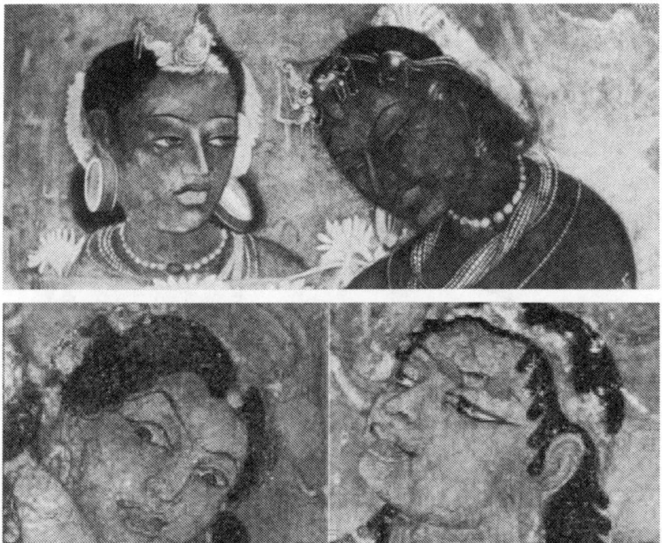

Frescos at Ajanta caves showing hairstyles of the period. Habibs curated a hugely popular show which demonstrated these coiffures on models

Habib, a famous judge at international events

Yes, hairdo that made heads turn. The event was a live depiction of ethnic hairstyles from the Ajanata and Elora frescoes which not only went on to prove that classical Indian beauties with long flowing tresses were more than capable of holding their own against present day trends, also that they could be back in vogue. Interwoven braids form highly ornate and intricate styles aptly titled *Jalpari* and *Shringaar*, the classical danseuse look where the hair is pined up in crescent shaped buns called the *ardh chandra* style, a figure of 8 ponytail, the *Matsyakanya* and a free flowing net like loose braid, the *Jhoola*, they were all there for the awed to behold.

'Each of these styles' takes hours to do. For each style, a number of accessories like jeweled clip beads, pearl pin and gold ribbons are used to enhance the final look. 'You cannot blindly imitate the West. One has to develop the level of creativity which may suit the Indian fashion and compliment the hair quality, texture and physical feature that Indians have', says the master stylist.

'The price of success is hard work, dedication to the job at hand, and the determination that whether we win or lose, we have applied the best of ourselves to the task at hand', Habib Ahmed adds.

Habib Ahmed became the hair stylist of the rich and the famous, with Gayatri Devi and Sam Manekshaw among his clients, within a very short time after his return from the UK. 'When my father came back to India from London, the

era was still of Raja, Maharajas who would come into big saloons in their fancy cars. Those people were obsessed with old traditions and they were hesitant about new looks. But when they came to discuss about their hair, they became even more traditional. My father kept negotiating and bargaining with them constantly to implement his ideas. Those Rajas had big heads and long hair and did not want to make them short', Amjad recalls.

GAYATRI DEVI

Somewhere Habib had understood that learning was the key and it also gives one the required exposure. 'Gayatri Devi took time to develop trust in me but when she did, she supported me like anything. She not only facilitated my course in Paris, but also paid for it without even letting me know the exact cost of the course. Later on, I found out the cost of the course but was told not to discuss it with the Maharani', recalls Habib.

Once, when the ageing Maharani was getting her haircut at the Habibs' Lodhi Hotel saloon, Habib Ahmed's son, the US-trained hairstylist Jawed remarked that his father had given an outdated cut to the Maharani's hair. At this, Gayatri Devi cast a cold look at Jawed and asked Habib to go on with his job.

'After I had finished, Gayatri Devi brushed the hair form her shoulders and quizzed Jawed about his training in the US. Then she said, "Jawed, your father has given me many

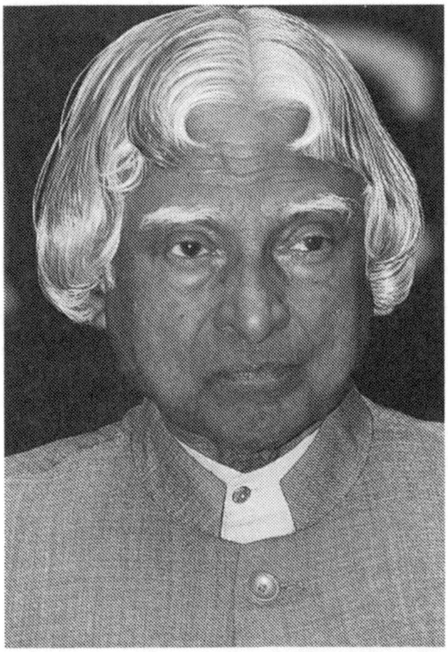

haircuts. If he puts the scissors to my hair, then please note that it is I who has asked him to cut the hair in this way. He does not style my hair out of his designs; he does it according to my wish." This royal retort silenced Javed', a smiling Habib Ahmed reminiscences.

REMEMBERING MISSILE MAN

Missile man APJ Abdul Kalam was among Habibs' famous clients. 'Abdul Kalam wanted the look of a philosopher. When Kalam shifted to Delhi in the late '90s, he visited Habibs' saloon at Lodhi Hotel for the first time. His hair was slightly longer than what was the fashion then', recalls Habib Ahmed, who became the hairdresser of the former President since then. 'But Kalam always wanted to sport that length. He was particular about that'. Kalama's iconic steel grey locks parted at the centre, with short half moon kiss curls on his forehead and longer length around the nape was his own typical style, quite oblivious of the trend at the time.

Habib recalls that every month, the smiling scientist would walk into his saloon. I used to take his opinion after trimming his hair. He loved his hair long and asked me not to cut it short. As his hairdresser, many a times, Habib would suggest that Kalam change the style. When the suggestion came repeatedly during his monthly trips to the saloon, Kalam decided to give it a try, respecting the wishes of Ahmed. 'I changed his style by keeping the

parting slightly off centre and reducing the length', Habib recollects. 'But Kalam was not amused. He was very much upset with the style I gave and showed some displeasure but in his own inimitable style, very politely, without sounding harsh.' Since nothing much could be done to get back the old style, Kalam wore the hair in that manner for some time, almost four months. Later he walked into Habib's saloon and said, 'I have grown my hair. Give it the same shape like the one it used to be.' The steely grey locks had gone dry and rough by now. So Ahmed offered the former President a serum to smoothen it. 'Kalam used it regularly and was happy with the sheen it gave to his hair', says Habib.

Due to the strategic nature of his job, Kalam always had high security around him, and he usually came to the saloon secretly in the evening. Soon after being nominated as the presidential candidate, Kalam paid a discreet visit to Habib's saloon. The news got leaked to the media and pressmen gathered outside Lodhi Hotel in large numbers. Kalam apparently did not like the exposure and stopped coming to Habibs after that. He, however, invited Habib and his family for tea at the Rashtrapati Bhavan after becoming President.

Did the former President talk about his faith which he shared with Habib Ahmed? Kalam often said, 'Khuda has given everything that is in Nature and that we, as human beings, should learn from Nature'. The conversations were always in English. 'Oh, sometimes he would start the conversations in Hindi and then soon lapse into English. He would say, 'My Hindi is weak'. And during his next visit he would again launch into Hindi for a while and say, 'My Hindi is slightly better than before' then smile at his inability to hold the conversation in Hindi for long and lapse into English again, recalls Ahmed fondly.

Kalam, the scientist, was a revered man and so Habib felt uncomfortable charging him for his services. 'I considered it a privilege to groom the hair of someone of Kalam's stature', he says. But Kalam was clear that he would not have any services gratis. He made his stand clear to Ahmed and said that he would be forced not to visit his saloon if he did not charge for the service he renders. 'He paid the amount for the haircut and did not ever ask for a discount.'

President Kalam was a very fine human being, soft at heart and down to earth always, in spite of his status and busy schedule. Once, when Kalam walked into the saloon for his monthly haircut, he was told that Habib Ahmed was hospitalised for some ailment. From the lobby of the hotel itself he called up Habib and enquired about his health. 'He spoke with me for half an hour. That was special as Dr Kalam was a very busy man. Yet, he took the time off to ask about my well being.'

Another time when Kalam was travelling in his car, he saw Habib Ahmed's car at a distance. He put out his hand and waved at them. Today Habib often remembers his meetings and conversation with Kalam and those memorable and precious moments spent with him, closeted well in the innermost chamber of his heart. He wonders how a person of such a stature could be that simple.

When Kalam became the President, the official hairstylist at Rashtrapati Bhavan was in charge of the President's haircuts. But the former President did not forget the former hair stylist. He invited Habib Ahmed and his family—children and grandchildren, to the Rashtrapati Bhavan. The office had given the Ahmed family just ten minutes time for the audience, but Kalam spent fortyfive minutes with them.

When at the Rashtrapati Bhavan, Habib Ahmed asked Kalam how he spent his evenings there. 'I say my isha namaz (late evening prayers) and then listen to south Indian classical music. Sometimes, I play the veena', Kalam told him. Habib then asked Kalam why he had never married. 'I was married', Kalam said jokingly. Then he smiled and said, 'I was married to the missile'.

'I had the great fortune to meet a scientist who became the President. After that, I could meet him only after he had relinquished his office. He was the same warm and caring person, no airs, no arrogance. When we met after Dr Kalam finished his tenure, he told me, ' Let's start our relationship again'. He meant, I could go back to cutting and styling his hair. But that day never came again, he was destined to leave us suddenly on a call from Khuda, as He required his company now!', Habib Ahmed says.

उदार नेहरू की कहानी हज्जाम की जुबानी

—जनक राज—

नजीर अहमद अपने आपको बहुत भाग्यशाली समझता है. बरसों से वह राष्ट्रपति भवन में हज्जाम का काम कर रहा है. इससे पहले उसके पिता, वाइसराय के यहां काम करते थे. नजीर अहमद देखने में तो काफी कम आयु के लगते हैं, परंतु इस समय उसकी आयु ५६ वर्ष की होगी.

१९४८ की बात है, पंडितजी और लार्ड माउंटबेटन शिमला (मशोबरा) गये थे. लार्ड माउंटबेटन नजीर अहमद को भी साथ ले गये थे. रात नौ बजे के बाद वे मशोबरा पहुंचे. वहां पर नजीर को पहली बार पंडितजी के बाल काटने का सौभाग्य प्राप्त हुआ. नजीर अहमद ने मुझे बताया कि जब बाल काटने के बाद वह बाहर आने लगा तो पंडितजी ने उसे कहा—'वेरी नाईस'

इस पर नजीर का कुछ हौसला बढ़ा और उसने साहस करके पंडितजी से कुछ बात करनी चाही. पंडितजी ने उसे कल आने के लिए कहा.

पंडितजी को हर बात का पूरा-पूरा ध्यान रहता था. उन्होंने अगले दिन हज्जाम, नजीर को स्वयं बुलाया और कहा कि बताओ तुम मुझ से कल क्या बात करना चाहते थे.

नजीर ने कहा, हुजूर बरसों से हमारा खानदान आप लोगों की खिदमत करता चला आ रहा है. मैं भी चाहता हूं कि आप लोगों के पांवों में पड़ा रहूं और आप लोगों की खिदमत करता रहूं. आजकल हवा भी खराब है—बाहर जाने को तबीयत नहीं करती—मैं हिंदुस्तान में ही रहना पसंद करूंगा.

पंडितजी ने नजीर से कहा कि आप घबराइए नहीं कुछ ही दिनों में हवा ठीक हो जायेगी. आप यहीं पर रहें. [illegible] बीच में बाल आ जाना. इस पर नजीर बहुत खुश हुआ और बदस्तूर पंडितजी के बाल काटता रहा. नजीर का कहना है कि बाल कटवाने के बाद पंडितजी अकसर कहा करते थे, 'शुक्रिया'.

बाल तो नजीर ने राजेंद्र बाबू और डा. राधाकृष्णन जी के भी बनाये, परंतु पंडितजी का यह लहजा—शुक्रिया—उसे बहुत पसंद आया और वह यह सुन-कर खुश हो जाता था.

एक बार नजीर अहमद की घड़ी खो गयी. बाल काटते-काटते नजीर ने पंडितजी से दबी जबान में कहा, 'हुजूर, मेरी तो घड़ी खो गयी'.

कुछ अरसा बाद जब पंडितजी यूरोप से लौटे, और नजीर अहमद जब बाल बनाने आया तो पंडितजी ने कहा—'यह लो, तुम्हारी अमानत' नजीर घड़ी को देखकर बहुत खुश हुआ और मन ही मन कहने लगा कि कहां मैं एक नाचीज और कहां यह हिंदुस्तान का मालिक-कितना ध्यान है हम छोटे लोगों का इनको'. यह बात कहते-कहते नजीर की आंखें छलछला आयीं.

नजीर ने पंडितजी से कहा कि वह इस बात को अखबार में देना चाहता है, परंतु पंडितजी ने कहा, 'नहीं-नहीं इसकी कोई जरूरत नहीं.'

यहीं नहीं-नजीर अहमद मरहूम को अकसर खाना पका कर खैरात किया करता था—पंडितजी से उसने कहा, 'हुजूर' आप भी कुछ मदद करें तो मेरा काम बन जायगा. पंडितजी ने उसी समय उसे १० रुपये दिलवा दिये. नजीर हालांकि राष्ट्रपति भवन में नौकर था परंतु लोग उसे पंडितजी का 'बारबर' (नाई) ही कहा करते थे.

नजीर अहमद अपनी दिक्कतें बाल काटते-काटते बताता रहता था. पंडित जी उसकी बड़े गौर से सुना करते थे. एक बार नजीर ने उन्हें बताया कि वह साबरिया खानदान का मुरीद है और खुदावंद ताला पर तवक्कल किये बैठा है. मगर महंगाई इस कदर है कि कुछ नहीं बना सका.

पंडितजी ने थोड़ा गुस्सा हो कर कहा, 'तुम क्या कहना चाहते हो.' नजीर ने बहुत नरमी से कहा, 'हुजूर रिटायर होने के बाद सोचता हूं कहां जाऊंगा—परिवार की नफरी भी कुछ ज्यादा है और गुजारा मुश्किल से होता है.' पंडित जी तुरंत पिघल गये और बोले, 'घबराओ मत, जो चाहोगे वही कर दिया जायगा.'

बस फिर क्या था, नजीर को तो ऐसा लगा कि खुदावंद ताला ने उस की सुन ली और वह जो चाहता था उसे मिल गया.

पंडितजी की बातें सुनाते-सुनाते नजीर कहने लगा, बाबूजी—वह तो कोई फरिश्ता था, इंसान नहीं—जितना भी उन के बारे में कहा जाय कम है.

एक बार नजीर पंडितजी के बाल न बना सका और इसी बीच में पंडितजी को रूस जाना पड़ गया. रूस से जब पंडितजी लौटे तो नजीर उन के बाल बनाने गया. बाल बहुत ही बढ़े हुए थे. नजीर ने उन से कहा, 'हुजूर बाल तो आप के बहुत बढ़ गए हैं.' पंडितजी ने बड़े ही मजाक के लहजे में कहा, 'यह तुम्हारी ही तो नालायकी का सबूत है, हमारे रूस जाने से पहले तुम ने हमारे बाल बनाये ही नहीं. आप को पता है कि मेरे बाल बारीक हैं और आप ही इस से वाकिफ हैं, इसलिए मैंने वहां बाल नहीं बनवाये.'

नजीर को पंडितजी बहुत ही प्यार करते थे और बच्चों की तरह उस से गुस्सा भी कर लेते थे. पंडितजी की

JAWAHARLAL NEHRU

Delving into memory lane, Habib remembers that Nazir Ahmed, his father, often narrated Panditji's stories. He once told him that Nehru knew that barbers often felt hesitant when their scissors come close to his ears, he used to often fold his ears during a haircut. Imagine a Prime Minister himself helping his barber. Habib grew up with many such stories.

It was a regular day, but that day Nazir Ahmed was not well and there were continuous calls from the Teen Murti Bhavan where the Prime Minister lived. The Prime Minister of India wanted a haircut only from Nazir. But Nazir was unwell. Then finally, Nazir took a chance and sent his 13-year-old son Habib Ahmed.

After a few minutes Habib was let inside the Teen Murti Bhavan. His hands were shaking, the reason being, there was a thin margin between his temple and his ears and these ears were none other than the ears of Pandit Jawaharlal Nehru.

'Nehruji thought that as a child I did not know much, so he would fold his ears to protect himself from cuts, and thereby help me in my work. Cutting his hair was tough as it spread like a rim around his head and it had to be cut evenly.' Nehru would calm a scared Habib and ask him to relax. The result was good. The basic lesson Habib learnt was that it is all about practice and the vision that one wants to achieve but, above all the confidence. This is one

Nehru & The Barber

DURING his brief visit to Delhi last week Lord Mountbatten ran into many old friends among the mourners at Prime Minister's House. One of them was Nazir Ahmed Salmani, the barber, who was on his personnal staff when he was here as Britain's last Viceroy. On leaving Delhi, Lord Mountbatten had recommended Nazir to Mr. Nehru and, except on one occasion when the Prime Minister was on a long visit to the Soviet Union, he cut Mr. Nehru's hair regularly during the past 16 years.

According to Nazir, Mr. Nehru spent most of his time in the barber's chair lost in deep thought—so deep sometimes that Nazir had to shake him out of his reverie. In time an attachment grew up between the two. On one of his visits abroad Mr. Nehru brought back a wristwatch for Nazir which he still wears and on the occasion of his daughter's wedding sent him a congratulatory letter with Rs. 50 enclosed. The last gift he got from Mr. Nehru was Rs. 10 to celebrate Moharrum. Nazir, who belongs to a family of barbers that started serving British viceroys from 1904, says that the most remarkable quality of Mr. Nehru was his politeness. He never forgot to say "shukriya" after he had dressed his hair and always apologised if he happened to be late for an appointment. While others, more highly placed than Nazir, will remember Mr. Nehru for other things, he will always remember him, he says, for his "graciousness."

of Habib Ahmed's proudest memories. 'He always greeted me with how are you? And at the finish would always say "thank You."'

'One day, my father got late going to Teen Murti Bhavan. But with even his best effort he couldn't reach Teen Murti Bhavan on his old bicycle on time. Nazir Ahmed was five minutes late. Even if it was five minutes, but for a Prime minister, it was a long time. Nehru seemed calm and said nothing to Nazir. After Nazir had cut his hair, Nehru asked in a low pitch, "Nazir! Why are you late today?" Nazir was speechless; he knew that it was his mistake. He then said, "I apologies for being late today, but the reason was that I don't have any watch. That is why it happened today. I promise that it will not happen again in the future." After a few days Nehru had occasion to visit the Soviet Union. When he came back from his visit, he sent a messenger to Nazir Ahmed to meet him. This time Nazir was not late. He came on time and met the Prime Minister.

'Panditji was smiling when he saw Nazir. He took a packet from the table and gave it to Nazir. Nazir was really surprised. He asked, "*Huzoor, ye kaya hai* (what is this sir)?" Nehru again smiled and said, "open it first". Nazir was overwhelmed and said nothing. It was a wrist watch, which the Prime Minister had brought for him form the Soviet Union. Nazir, on his way home on his bicycle kept thinking, "that day I was late due to my miscalculation of time, but I made an excuse in front of Nehruji, that I don't

have watch. But Nehruji noticed this and kept it in mind."
'Pandit Nehru was like our family member, we were very close to the Nehru family. On every festive occasion my father and our whole family used to go to Teen Murti Bhavan. Nehruji admired my father very much. He could have easily appointed another barber as well, but he always insisted my father cut his hair', says Habib.

CHARLES AND DIANA

In April 1981, Prince Charles was getting married to Lady Diana. By that time, Diana was a style icon. Habib's watchful eyes were always on the top guys. A little before the wedding, Habib wrote to Charles, suggesting a slight change in his hair style which he felt could result in giving his face, 'a much softer look'. He added that the Prince's hair ought to be styled in steps all around for the requisite effects. Charles' secretary wrote to say that the Prince was grateful for the stylist's thoughtfulness. By looking at Prince Charles' later photographs Habib noticed a slight change along the lines suggested by him.

In one of the Newspaper interviews in 2005, Habib was asked a question, 'which is the most popular hair style that he recommended to his clients?' Habib replied that, 'while the style depends on face cuts and body structure as also hair type, I would say the one style that has become internationally popular is the original layered look that Lady Diana sported at the time of her wedding. This has been the

most copied look and even today, in India people often go in for the layered look with steps at above the shoulder level. I once had a lady come in and request for the style and I was nonplussed because she was ugly, short and plump with a strong jawline which would just not go with the cut. It took me a long time to persuade her not to go in for the Lady Diana look that she so desperately wanted.'

There is mathematics involved in hair styling. Hair has a mathematical and geometrical calculation, which should blend well with the complexion and personality. An expert hair stylist will always go in for all these calculation to give you the right cut. Charlie Chaplin said once that, 'fools and artist are born, not made'. Habib repeatedly emphasises that 'Hair styling is an art that only a few have managed to acquire despite the fact that hair saloons have mushroomed in every corner'.

Gone are the days when you just snipped and trimmed the locks to make it presentable. Now people are more aware of the texture, the style and yes even colours of the hair. In fact, for Habib Ahmed it is a science. The efforts he has put in the business has made him a household name. A successful hair stylist is not one who can snip the locks with abandon but one who can match the style equally with the facial contours and Habib does just that. Habib's endeavour has always been to bring out the client's personality when he styles a person's hair. He tries to match the style to the age, profession, lifestyle, status and most importantly, to

the time they give to preening themselves. The hair style that Habib gives one depends on one's face cut, height, figure, as much as on the hair texture.

IMRAN KHAN

A framed photograph featuring a famous face reminds us of one of Habib Ahmed's earliest triumphs. In the photograph, you may have noticed how his hair is short in the front and long at the back. Pointing to the appropriate part of the picture, Habib senior explains, 'He has a wide jaw, squarish. His hair is naturally wavy. That is why I gave him that style. So that when he ran up to bowl, the longer hair at the back provided ample body for his strong jaw line, and the wavy hair reminded the audience of his bounce like the bounce of a stallion in full flow'. This became Imran Khan's hallmark in India.

THE IRON LADY

Habib had known Indira from his childhood as his father was hairdresser to Nehru, who used to get his haircut in the backyard of Teen Muriti Bhavan. In the early days of Independence, Muslim employees of Rashtrapati Bhavan used to observe Milad-e-Sharif, and Indira was a regular at the evening programmes. 'The world remembers only the powerful Indira Gandhi. But I have seen her attend Milad-e-Sharif at Rashtrapati Bhavan long before she was poliically active. She was a soft-spoken person', Habib recalls.

'*Yeh bataon, London se kya teer maar kar aye ho* (What is the big deal you have learnt in London)?', Indira Gandhi once joked. In 1970, Habib took off for a course at Vidal Sasoon's saloon in London. Two years later, Indira got the first London-trained hairdresser in Delhi to cut her hair. Indira was very familiar with the Western world, and she also knew that Habib had done hair dressing courses form London.

Habib fondly remembers Indira Gandhi. 'She was so simple and humble, one could not even guess, she was the Prime Minister. I used to go at 7 o' clock in the morning to give her a hair cut, she would wake up fresh like a flower, waiting with a warm smile on her face.'

It was Habib's biggest break, when Indira asked him to be her hair dresser after she became Prime Minister and her regular hairdresser Sabri went off to London. Dressing Indira's hair was not an easy job, Habib was not sure if he could satisfy the PM. He was planning to do something different but Habib was not sure what he was going to do. Habib told us with a sparkle in his eyes that 'Indiraji never asked me for any specific style of hair, she always told me "*jaisa thik samajhiye kijiye* (do whatever you feel is right)."'

Usually Habib got a call in the evening form the Prime Minister's Residence, and the frequency was about ten to fifteen days. Indira knew Habib must have been very busy during the daytime, so she called him only in the evenings. Everyone knows that Indira's trademark was her hair and managing and styling this kind of hair was complex. Habib

settled the hair neatly and made it look stylish but at the same time did not let it spike. The Prime minister of India always had paucity of time, but she never asked Habib to hurry. During cutting or trimming the hair, Indira's daughter-in-law always stayed close by keeping a close watch on what was going on. Habib remembers this as a positive intervention as getting Soina's advises was always welcomed. He was not keen on changing Indira's overall style.

Habib also admits that somewhere he was also scared of changing the style. Basically, the idea was clear in Habib's mind, he knew that Indiraji could not afford much time every day on hair styling, so the priority was to style her hair in such a fashion that she could carry it off with dignity suited to the office of a PM. At the same time, it had to be something she could do herself and in the least time.

During the cutting sessions Indira often wore a 'Kashmiri Shawl' over her sari. At times she would talk about her hair, some contemporary issues and sometime didn't like to say a single word and sat with her eyes closed. Habib preferred to cut hair while it was wet as it was easy to manage. He remembers that once Indiraji told him to cut her hair without getting them wet, as it would take too much to get them dry. She admitted that she did not get time to set her hair during the day, so she just washed her hair and wrapped it in a net before sleeping.

In the 1950s, Indira Gandhi had sported plain middle-parted hair, pulled back into a knot at the back. At the start

of the 1960s, she swapped to a Bouffant-ish style, which was in vogue and also made her nose appear less protruding.

When Indira Gandhi's hair started greying she travelled to Paris for a makeover. The fashion of the day was to have a pile of hair on top. Indira, an exception, wore her hair short. This brought Habib into the picture in India. There was a lot of secrecy over Indira's hairstyle, and Habib knew them all. 'A top hairdresser in Paris gave her the first haircut that made her famous.' Habib remembers that 'My job was to preserve that look. I was asked not to discuss it with anyone. Indiraji had curly hair, and long hair did not suit her at all', he says. Indira's hair had turned all grey by the end of her first term in office. 'It was then that I carried a German dye to her house on 1, Safdarjung Road. She was adamant on paying for the expensive dye, but Habib was hesitant to charge her. Finally, Habib charged her Rs 25 so that she did not feel bad.

Habib had the difficult task of adding a touch of elegance to the mass of white hair on Indira's scalp. 'I thought that a white patch should be left without the dye, to add to her elegance', Habib Ahmed says. The media at the time reported, 'Indira's signature black and white hairstyle became her political trademark. It is believed that a famous Parisian hairstylist was responsible for her selective graying. Her significant hairdo inspired many women of her era, who sported similar hairstyle complete with the grey streak.'

Habib says he had a flair for words and during his stay in London, he had worked hard on his English accent.

'For hours, I would speak looking into the mirror, but working with political personalities made me understand the importance of silence. We were told that you should not speak or indulge in talk about any other thing, other than your field of expertise. Once, after a party, I revealed to a few journalists the secret of the white patch on Indira Gandhi's hair and it didn't go down well with the lady. It was the creation of a French coiffeur which I had to learn.'
However, in the same breath, he tells us how he put his knowledge of Urdu to good use once, when Indira was about to go to address a rally at Nizamuddin and was struggling to find the right translation for a few words.
Habib found Indira's house a political battlefield as everyone jostled to get her attention. There was Dhirendra Brahmachari, The Prime Minister's yoga instructor, who could not be antagonised; then there was a coterie of Indira's servants and assistants. 'Nathu, the son of a gardener at Teen Murti Bhavan, had become very powerful under the circumstances. Next was RK Dhawan', recalls Habib. Once Indira had to dye her hair late in the evening for an early morning function, but Habib was not available that morning. The next morning, he found that Nathu, Indira's aide, had applied two coats of the German dye on the Prime Minister's hair, and the double dyeing left Indira's scalp dry and itchy. Habib told Nathu not to do this as it could be injurious, and Nathu was furious. 'Recounting that incident', Habib says, 'I understood then it was not

easy to be in the house of the Prime Minister. I needed to show respect to everybody so that no one around Mrs Gandhi misunderstood my good intentions.' Sometimes he would be summoned right before a press conference, because one of Indira's aides would have spotted a strand of hair that might have looked out of place on camera.

Sonia Gandhi never came to him for a haircut, he says, but Maneka came to him sometimes. He suggested she perm her poker-straight hair and she told him that even her husband had suggested it. She booked an appointment to get it done, but a week prior to it, Sanjay Gandhi died. She came very occasionally after that, though her son Varun gets his hair cut by Habib Ahmed's son, Jawed. Habib saab has seen Varun play on Sonia's lap.

'When I met Indira Gandhi after I returned from abroad, she told me to spread my knowledge to Indians but those were the days when women loved wearing their hair in a bun and I had no clue how to do it. As a creative hair stylist, I wanted to cut the hair but no lady was interested in short hair. They were almost paranoid about cutting the hair', is what Habib Ahmed tells us of the 1970s.

THE POWERFUL

Habib does not tell his students and staff about his association with distinguished clients. The list includes names such as VV Giri and Zakir Hussain.

Zakir Hussain, who was known to be close to Indira Gandhi, used to get his trademark French beard trimmed twice a week. Habib remembers that Dr Hussain would get grumpy if the garden of his porch was not looked after well. Trimming his beard in those grumpy spells was tough, Habib recollects.

Cutting Giri's hair gave Habib a chance to become hairdresser to members of the President's family, especially his daughter Mohini Giri. Once Mohini's personal aide called out saying, '*Nai aya hai* (the barber has come). Mohini later apologised for her staffer's rudeness. But it was during this time that Habib realised that despite his high-end and exclusive clients, he was far from enjoying respect in society. His search for dignity and social outreach won him the admiration of many including the current Rajya Sabha member Mohammed Adeeb and his family. Says Adeeb: 'Habib got his profession by virtue of tradition, but he improved and innovated on it.'

BOLLYWOOD GREATS

'I have been grooming actors and models along with my son Jawed and they are all very particular about looking good', Habib Ahmed says, remembering his Bollywood clients. 'Rajesh Khanna was my favourite', he says. 'Even old timers like Dilip Kumar have stopped oiling their hair and now pay more attention to their hair style if not anything else.'

'Dilip Kumar and Raj Kapoor had similar hair styles—combed back with a slight quaff, which was the rage after films like *Mughal-e-Azam*, *Shree 420* and *Awaara*. The quaff gave a wavy effect on the forehead. But unlike today, actors then used to apply oil to their hair.'

'The Sadhana cut was no great piece of hair styling. It became popular just because of an actress. The people who used to come to me earlier had risen above the fascination for Bollywood actors, so I was not inundated by demands of following a particular actor's cut. Amitabh Bachchan's mother used to come to me and was a little finicky about the styling.'

Pooja Bedi with Habib and Jawed

Vyjayanthimala releasing Habib's CD

Rajesh Khanna inaugurating a Habib saloon

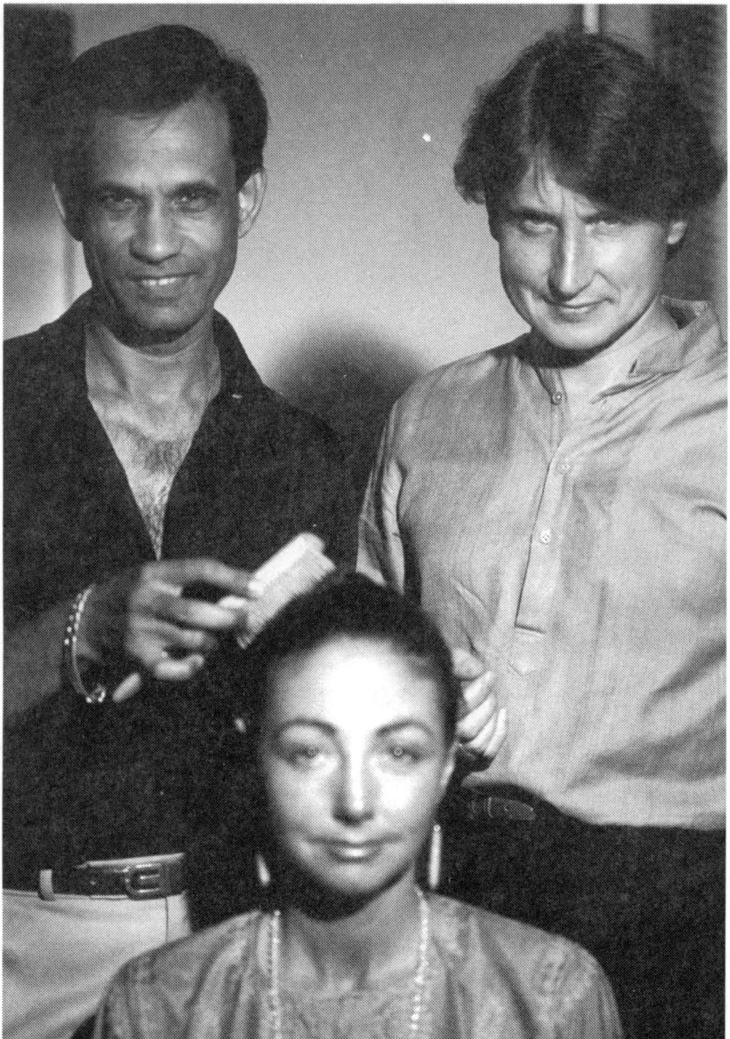

Habib with Horst at Oberoi 1986

Rekha: She has long wavy hair. To have her hair styled to suit every dress and role, she should trim her hair slightly at the back and have a few short wisps on the forehead. (Parvez recalls that Rekha was their client in the days of his father when paying a tip of Rs 2/- was the done thing, and she payed as much).

IMRAN KHAN
Present and recommended hairstyle

Imran Khan: We styled his hair in a style that suits a sportsman perfectly—cut short in front so as to not come into the eyes and long and light at the back. They swing when he's in action.

Sharon Prabhakar: She's got a beautiful style and she maintains it perfectly.

Dimple Kapadia: She had got the best style I have ever seen. Her bleached streaks look really good. Now, of course, she's changed her style to a bob-cut.

Vyjanthimala: Gets her hair done in long steps at Habib's now. It makes her look younger and she is very happy.

Princess Diana: She has a perfect style. And it's a very difficult cut from the point of view of a hair dresser.

SONIA GANDHI
Present and recommended hairstyle.

Sonia Gandhi: She should get her wavy thick hair cut in long steps, with first step on front reaching upto her collar bone. She can, then, pin the first step away from her hair when in formal political circles and look comfortable and elegant with them down otherwise.

Vijay Amritraj: He's got curly, kinky hair. They should be cut with a razor to avoid the kinky look and be kept long.

Sunil Gavaskar: He must dye his hair to a darkish brown colour leaving the side burns grey (like Pataudi). The length of the hair should be kept short as they are very frizzy.

Kapil Dev: His side burns should not be shaved off. The hair style should be like that of Imran Khan.

ingredients or that is in any way sore, scratched or infected. Perming is good for oily hair because, besides giving it a volume, the lift of the hair helps to prevent the sebum travelling up the shaft very quickly. After-perm treatment should consist of using gentle shampoos and plenty of conditioners to counteract any adverse effects.

Of course, any chemical treatment is bad. So I prefer to make hair do with a cut whenever it is possible to avoid a perm.

Talking of dyes, in India, the range of synthetic dyes is very limited. A truly herbal dye is not available. Most of the synthetic dyes do not give a natural look to the hair. It is better to blend shades to get the natural shade. Streaking is a very good way of highlighting hair. However, the dye should first be tested for allergy. Henna is an excellent natural hair-dye in use since Indus Valley Civilisation. Besides adding rich red tones, henna also conditions the hair, giving it an extra lustre.

Ques: *How can hair be conditioned ?*

Ans: Besides using the synthetic cream rinse or conditioner after every shampoo, vinegar or lemon juice can be added to the final rinsing water.

THE SCIENTIFIC ANGLES

The hair root is the fastest-growing organ in the body: the hair on the scalp, for example grows at an average rate of 1/2 an inch a month. Hair does not grow at a constant rate. It's growth is seasonal—it grows faster in summer months than in winters. Secondly, hair does not grow indefinitely. The growth phase for each individual hair varies from person to person. It generally lasts for between 2-6 years—but it may go on for much longer, as the fact that people have hair long enough to sit on indicates. When the growth phase ends, the hair follicle enters the resting period for a few months. It stops getting longer and remains till a new hair forms underneath and pushes it out.

Natural hair colour and all other characteristics of hair growth, such as curliness, oiliness and thickness, are hereditary. It is possible to change the appearance of your hair by using an artificial colourant. A chemical film is applied to the hair shaft. The depth to which the dye penetrates into the hair shaft determines how long the artificial colour lasts. Some colourants shampoo out within weeks; others change colour permanently, until the hair is cut off.

Appearance of hair can also be changed by perm. A perm operates by rehardening should shampooing leave the hair 'squeaky clean' (i.e. too much oil and moisture having been removed). Brush your hair thoroughly before shampooing to loosen dirt and dead skin cells from the scalp. Wet the hair, work a teaspoonful of shampoo into the strands and rinse till every trace of shampoo is removed. Repeat shampooing if necessary.

Ques: *How can split-ends be prevented ?*

Ans: Hair should be trimmed regularly to avoid split-ends. Oil massage prevents further splitting. In case of split ends all along the length, trimming professionally is essential.

Ques: *Is blow drying safe and how is it best done?*

Ans: It's safe if done at the most twice a week at well-controlled temperatures. Avoid using hot air. Low or cool is the right temperature.

It is not necessary to use much shampoo to get good results, nor should shampooing leave the hair 'squeaky clean'. Brush your hair thoroughly before shampooing to loosen dirt and dead skin cells from the scalp.

Bouncy looks, straight or curled can be achieved through blow-drying—but only if the dryer is safely used at a distance of at least 15 cm from the hair and moved rapidly over each section to avoid dehydration.

Roughly blow-dry all hair till only slightly damp. Using the tail of the comb divide hair into sections according to curls or separate into upper, lower, side and back sections. Dry the lower back and side sections first, then do the upper back and side sections. Blend all sections together. Dry a fringe last.

Ques: *Is perming and hair-dyeing safe?*

Ans: Both these processes, with the exception of the temporary water-colour rinses, involve long-term change in the appearance, enlivening the dullest, drabbest and most unmanageable hair.

For perming, hair should always be trimmed for a permanent wave treatment. Using a perm on hair that is already broken or damaged may cause it all to break off close to the scalp. Perm should never be used on a scalp that is sensitive to strong

Being Trendy

Just as a good frame enhances the beauty of a picture, so does a good hairstyle highlight the beauty of a face. It is the jewel of a person's personality. Here Parvej talks of the latest style and what he thinks would suit some of our celebrities

His: Long hair on the top and shorter on the sides and back.

Her: Short on the top and long enough to be tied at the back.

AMITABH BACHCHAN
Present and recommended hairstyle

RAJIV GANDHI
Present and recommended hairstyle.

Rajiv Gandhi: His hair should be kept a little longer because this short hair with a balding top makes him look balder. His side-burns should be short and undyed and the rest of the hair be dyed in a balanced light shade (very dark hair do not go with his fair ruddy complextion). Also, the dye should be put more frequently and equally on both sides of the head, for now there are patches of dark and light in his hair at times. He should also trim his eyebrows a bit.

Amitabh Bachchan: His side-burns should be short, his hair should cover half his ears and be slightly longer at the back. His parting should not be very visible.

Of locks & looks

Most people blindly follow elders in the family when it comes to styling their hair. But, says HABIB AHMED, one of the pioneers of hair styling in India, a good and suitable hair style can do wonders to one's personality.

A simple hairstyle enhances one's personality.

ONCE a young girl accompanied by her mother approached me through a friend. She wanted to know if I could help her improve her personality as a young man ,was coming to see her for matrimonial alliance. Despite her young age she was an ordinary looking girl with straight long hair. She had been rejected on earlier occasions on this count and didn't want to face the same situation this time. After trying a couple of hair-styles, I gave her one which suited her perfectly well. She left the place quite happy and satisfied. Few days later she rang up to tell me that she would be getting married very soon.

A good and suitable hairstyle can do wonders to one's personality. For this, consideration of an individual's face, figure and built are a must. When someone approaches me for a hair style, I have a good look at the face before deciding which style would suit the person best. In fact with me a wrong hairstyle becomes a major irritant. Sometimes I stop people on the way and suggest a particular hairstyle to enhance their personality.

What perturbs me most is the fact that very few Indians in the profession are really trained for the job. Often people who visit a well known beauty parlour do so for the satisfaction of having been there.

The common attitude is to ask for the hairstyle of a particular film star or alternatively whatever is in fashion, without caring whether or not it would suit them. Sometimes the order is — "Please do not cut my hair". They do not understand that no styling is possible without cuts.

Besides, the length of hair from the point where it starts thinning is of no use. The hair from this point is generally under-nourished and unhealthy. Trimming such hair once in six weeks is a must.

I have never been able to understand the craze for hair dyes and rinses. With natural hair conditioners and local dyes like henna being easily available we should avoid using chemicals. I recommend a good shampoo as a substitute for beer. Also I am not in favour of using hair rollers etc. A good hair style should be such that the cut remains unchanged after shampoo and brushing. There should be no need for setting or blow-drying. In today's busy life style people essentially prefer a hairstyle that does not have to be set every week. For them I advise a cut that just falls into shape. Called the Wedge cut with five geometrical lines, the accent is on naturalness.

The problem with most Indians is their rigidity to part with long hair even if it is unhealthy. Such people are never convinced about a change and would like to continue the style they have been using since their childhood. With gentle persuasion I have been able to convince quite a few of them. Most of the time they have been a lot more happy with the result.

I have adopted different styles to go with different dresses. For instance I do not approve of hair above the shoulder for sari-clad women.

To help women avoid ruining their hair we need more hairstyling courses in the country. Such courses could be started as part of arts and crafts in the school curriculum. This will improve the technical standards in the profession and offer better job opportunity to educated youngsters.

Heir-raising story

HABIB is streaking these days. Not racing around in the buff as the phrase used to mean in the seventies, but colouring his hair, to keep up with the rephrased version of the eighties. Delhi's first, last and middle name in hair-dressing has added streaks of yellow, red and green to his crowning glory.

Visitors to his salop at Lodhi Hotel now have two sights to gulp at. One is his hair and the other, the bill for a haircut at the hands of the hairdresser who drops the names of Vidal Sassoon and Robert Fielding like so many pins on his polished floor.

Also a part of his crowning glory, if not exactly a part of his coiffure are his two sons, who have just returned from London and are being introduced to clients and the business. To ensure that your hair today can be styled by tomorrow's heirs.

Me Myself

Talking about himself, Habib saab says that for the past many years, he has been busy travelling. 'I am always going to Hong Kong or New York or some other places to attend conferences and meets to act as a judge in competitions, to do refresher courses. I hardly have time for anything but my work.'

'But when I am here (in Delhi), I generally wake up at six in the morning and do some exercise. I am very particular about my shaving. I can't remember a single day when I've skipped shaving, read the papers and spend at least half an hour reading books on hairstyling, on new innovations like streaking the hair for instance. I have a very light breakfast and then go to the school.'

'I love speaking to my students. Then I go to the shop where I have a really busy schedule. I think Indians have the best hair texture in the world. Indians are yet not very willing to experiment on the hair. I hardly get time for lunch. But

I enjoy my dinner. Sitting with family together and eating. I watch a little TV and go to bed by about twelve. Again I spend some time on reading books about hairdressing. But at the moment I am obsessed with the idea of doing something in the field—of bringing in more professionals, by training and raising the standards, creating more awareness, of doing a good show—of putting India on the world map.'

'Now in the last phase of my life, I am still fully active. But there has always been a flicker that has always haunted me—that there is something more in this life besides my work. I should think about this and work upon this. The fact is that till now I couldn't get time to anlayse this feeling and thought. Let us see when that time will arrive.'

Around year 2002, when I met with the famous painter MF Hussain, I was an amateur theatre activist and I was one of the actors of the theatre group called IPTA, which was doing a play based on Hussain's biography. During preparations I got the opportunity to interact with him. I asked him a question. 'Did you find a sense of spirituality in your work?' MF said, 'Yes, off course. Many times when I was fully into my colours and canvas, I entered in another world, where I need not think about shades of colour, shapes and other things. At that point of time I felt that someone was guiding me, my brush just moved according to that heavenly will.' Further he added that everyone in his life or work gets this opportunity to be lost somewhere in spirituality. And today when I am writing this book, I am in search of that element of spirituality in Habib too. But why is it so? Because this is for sure that no one can reach so far in his career, until and unless he has some strong inner power or one can say inner motivation.

It was in year 2004, during a charity programme, that Habib Ahmed met Archana Didi, the well-known spiritual guru based in Delhi. At the tender age of 4 years, a blessed child was found immersed in deep silence and meditation. Archana Didi's family, neighbours and all the people around were amazed to find such a small child with a 'God Persona'. The teachers in school were also overwhelmed by the aura of this sacred child. In a very short time everyone around her realised that she was indeed a gifted child. Over time, this gifted child with her continuous and arduous meditation and divine grace of her spiritual master attained enlightenment at an early age and was anointed as a 'Sadguru', Meditation Guru. When Habib met her, he just expressed his thoughts about his training programme for marginalised people and future course of action.

'What is spirituality? It is just hearing of your inner voice and this voice is beyond of words, religion.' Archana Didi was stunned how a man who was a big name in his field, 'a man who was an icon in the whole world as far as hair styling in India is concerned, wanted to give his knowledge to coming generations. And this man was so humble and down to earth.' Habib's simplicity touched Archana Didi. Didi recalls how she just described success and this act of giving to others as his inner voice, which can lead to god. She put forward a few points before Habib. 'You can hear God's voice as part of a growing conversational relationship with him. Many people would say they try to listen to God.

But there is much confusion on discerning if you've truly heard God's voice. I know people who were sure they had heard God's voice and so they acted on it only to discover down the road that they were being impulsive. Hearing God as a reliable, day-to-day reality for people with good sense', and it is possible, she told Habib.

'The Inner Voice is the heart's wealth. When an aspirant uses this wealth, it soulfully smiles. When an unbeliever and disbeliever in God attempts to use this wealth, it is mercilessly suffocated. The Inner Voice tells us to help the world only in accordance with God's express Will. If help is rendered otherwise, it is bound to turn into dire calamity later on. He is not only divinely liberal but supremely blessed whose help to another is God inspired and God-ordained', Habib today echoes the spiritual leader.

'I want to do something new and fascinating, actually I want to grow. I think I always had in my mind that what life I have, I have to get out of it, and this is only me who can do this. I want to do something but don't know what', says Habib, adding, 'and I always recite these line of a sher:

> *Doobo de usko ya paar kar de ye teri marzi,*
> *Utha ke langar maine chod di tere sahare par*
> Drown him or get him to the banks, it's your wish, I have lifted the anchor of the boat and my fate is up to you.

'I got opportunity many time to visit Pakistan, and when I was in Lahore, I visited many times Iqbal sahib's mazar (grave), I am very fascinated with Iqbal sahib.Ghalib is also my all-time favourite poet, but I am not able to understand him completely. In the new age of shayari, I liked Rahat Indouri and Munnavar Rana', Habib saab tells us.

During the sittings for this book, I met Habib saab several times. One of the pleasures of meeting him is to hear some select sher.

> *Naa tha kuch to khuda tha kuch naa hota to khuda hota,*
> *Dooboya mujhko hone naa hota main to kya hota.*
> God was there when nothing existed; I lost myself
> to being something, if I had not existed, then what
> difference could it have made.

Habib saab told me, in 1979 he had bought a tape recorder. To have a tape recorder was great at that time. He is very fond to music, specially Ghazals. He played Ghazals and sufi music on the tape recorder, but this is not the story. Habib used this to record live performances of Ghazal concerts, individual performances and Mushaira. Sometimes, he literary carried his tape recorder and roamed the city of Delhi to find some gathering where his favouite poetry was being sung or recited.

Although, he himself does not write, Habib quotes Johann and says, 'Every day we should hear at least one little song, read one good poem, see one exquisite picture, and, if possible, speak a few sensible words.' One of his oldest associates Zameer Ahmed recalls those days and explains, how Habib saab was mad about poetry and whenever he got time he would rush away from his work for a sher shairi session somewhere. Habib justifies his passion, 'I am not very educated, as far as conventional education is concerned. But poetry gives me the depth to understand the mystery of life. It makes me cool and mature. Besides this, I want to know them closely, those people who have such a god's gift to create another world through words.'

Mat sahal hame jano firta hai falak barson,
Tab khaq ke parde se insaan niklte hain.
Don't think that it is easy to be a man, it takes years to become a real human.

Habib made many friends during his visits of music concerts, qawali and Mushairas. He found several such friends who had the same hobby to record live music or poetry narration. They exchanged audio tapes and shared their thoughts. One of his friends from that era, Maqbool, recall a story, when Habib Ahmed, a journalist and Maqbool himself were coming back from a Ghazal evening in Delhi. They were travelling in a car, and Habib played his tape recorder. The third person, that journalist, was really surprised and impressed. He asked for a copy of that recording of Ghazal performance, but Habib politely refused, saying that, 'there is only one copy and this is mine, so I will keep this'.

'Getting success from scratch is a wonderful thing, but I can say the passion to share success is greater. That is why Habib Ahmed is iconic.' When I heard these word from non other than Sudhir Tailang, who was himself an iconic artist, I knew I had to write about Habib saab.
The self-taught cartoonist reportedly started drawing at the age of five. By ten, his first cartoon was published. Sudhir helped me to understand why even today Habib saab is so

energetic. 'Life of Habib Ahmed has been full of struggle and also a success story of entrepreneurship. Today Habibs is a brand. But what he is doing now, he is sharing his skill and idea. That make him icon and also a man full of positive energy', Tailang told me.

Habib saab does not look his age. In his eight decade of this life, he is full of positivity and I think the source of this energy is hidden in sharing. Tailang, a much younger man who is no more, always tried to highlight why Habib saab should be recognised as a pioneer. 'He opted for this barber profession when society had a backward thinking over it. He then gave it a high value. Now it is a career option, a serious career option', said Sudhir remembering how it took many years to gain respect for Habib Ahmed's kind of work.

References

1. The Cutting Edge (*The Weekend Observer,* 5 Nov 1994)
2. Earl Helps Barber Habib to Brush up (*Sunday Mirror* London – 24-3-68)
3. The Viceroy's House (Rashtrapati Bhavan, by EL Lutyens: Part I-Jacqueline Banerjee, Associate Editor, the *Victorian Web*)
4. *Nai: Henna Artist: Central India*, 1910: RL Desai, Gwalior
5. Barbers and hairstylists, August 20, 2011, *The Hindu*
6. Earl Helps Barber Habib to Brush up (*Sunday Mirror* London – 24-3-68)
7. *Shear Joy! The Hindu* April 12, 2013
8. *The Sunday Observer* Life: August 15, 1993
9. A romance with hair styling (By Alka Saxena – 7-4-1982)

10. *Shear Joy! The Hindu* April 12, 2013
11. Cute hair style-Story behind Mrs. Gandhi's peculiar hairstyle and color? : September 3, 2015 in Blog
12. *Exotica*/November 2014
13. *Shear Joy! The Hindu* April 12, 2013
14. Snipping away the family division: Caroline D'Cruz, *Times of India*, May 29, 2012
15. *India today*,Generation why—Dilip Bobb, January 31, 2005
16. Identity crisis: Indian Youth-By Gayatri Sankar.
17. *Business today*—In your face:G. Seetharaman—Edition: Jan 22, 2012
18. April 2013: vccircle.com
19. The Hindustan Times 29, 1997
20. *What Is Beauty*—exampleeassy.com
21. Salon chain to train Tihar jail inmates: *Hindustan Times*, New Delhi, Jun 07, 2008
22. Tihar mein catwalk, *Times of India*, Aug 16, 2009
23. Hair Apparent!—*The Indian Express*, January 19, 2005.
24. *Afternoon Despatch & Courier,* Feb 27 2002
25. A life in the day of Habib: by Poonam Saxena
26. *The Hindustan Times*, October 29, 1997.